MW01706353

DETECTIVE STORY

ACTING EDITION

PLAY IN THREE ACTS

BY SIDNEY KINGSLEY

★

★

DRAMATISTS
PLAY SERVICE
INC.

Play by Sidney Kingsley; setting by Boris Aronson; costumes by Millie Sutherland; staged by Mr. Kingsley; first presented by Howard Lindsay and Russel Crouse at the Hudson Theatre, New York, March 23, 1949.

THE CAST

Joe Feinson .... Lou Gilbert
Detective Dakis .... Robert Strauss
Shoplifter .... Lee Grant
Detective Gallagher .... Edward Binns
Mrs. Farragut .... Jean Adair
Detective Callahan .... Patrick McVey
Detective O'Brien .... John Boyd
Detective Brody .... James Westerfield
Endicott Sims .... Les Tremayne
Detective McLeod .... Ralph Bellamy
Arthur Kindred .... Warren Stevens
Patrolman Barnes .... Early Sydnor
1st Burglar (Charlie) .... Joseph Wiseman
2nd Burglar (Lewis) .... Michael Strong
Mrs. Bagatelle .... Michelette Burant
Dr. Schneider .... Harry Worth
Lt. Monoghan .... Horace McMahon
Susan Carmichael .... Joan Copeland
Patrolman Keogh .... Byron C. Halstead
Patrolman Baker .... Joe Roberts
Willy .... Carl Griscom
Miss Hatch .... Maureen Stapleton
Mrs. Feeney .... Sarah Grable
Mr. Feeney .... Jim Flynn
Crumb-Bum .... Archie Benson
Mr. Gallantz .... Garney Wilson
Mr. Pritchett .... James Maloney
Mary McLeod .... Meg Mundy
Tami Giacoppetti .... Alexander Scourby
Photographer .... Michael Lewin
Lady .... Ruth Storm
Gentleman .... John Alberts
Mr. Bagatelle .... Joseph Ancona
Indignant Citizen .... Jacqueline Paige

TIME: The present.

The entire action of the play takes place in the detective squad room of a New York precinct police station.

ACT I. A day in August, 5:30 P. M.

ACT II. 7:30 P. M.

ACT III. 8:30 P. M.

DETECTIVE STORY

ACT I

AT RISE: *For details on the setting see frontispiece, and stage diagram on p. 96.* NICHOLAS DAKIS *is seated at typewriter* L.*—Desk No. 1—making out a form and interrogating a* WOMAN-SHOPLIFTER*—who has been picked up for shoplifting. At* C. *desk—Desk No. 2—his partner,* GALLAGHER, *is writing up some " squeals." Set clock 5:30.*

DAKIS. Eyes? (*Squints at* SHOPLIFTER'S *eyes.*)
SHOPLIFTER. (*Seated in chair above desk No. 1.*) Brown.
DAKIS. (*Typing.*) Hair?
SHOPLIFTER. Titian.
DAKIS. Red. (*Phone buzzer sounds.*)
GALLAGHER. (*Into phone.*) 21st Squad Detectives, Gallagher. Yes, madam? What is your name, please? Address? (*He reaches for pad, glances at clock, writes.*) Phone number? Plaza 9-1855. . . .
DAKIS. (*Types.*) Weight?
GALLAGHER. One second, please. (*Another buzzer sounds. Picks up other receiver, balancing first on his shoulder.*) 21st Squad, Detectives, Gallagher.
SHOPLIFTER. 109, I think.
DAKIS. (*Types.*) 109 will do. Height?
SHOPLIFTER. I don't know. About . . . (*Shrugs shoulders.*)
DAKIS. Stand up against the wall! Over there. (*Waves her to height chart on wall* R. *of fingerprint shelf. To* SHOPLIFTER.) Five one, all right, come back. (SHOPLIFTER *returns to Desk No. 1.*)
GALLAGHER. (*On phone.*) Hello, Loot. No, nothing. A shoplifter. Macy's. A pocketbook. (*Calls to* DAKIS.) Hey, Nick, what was the price on that purse she lifted?
SHOPLIFTER. Six dollars.
GALLAGHER. (*On phone.*) Six bucks.
DAKIS. Age?

SHOPLIFTER. 26—(*Corrects herself, quickly.*) 22.
DAKIS. (*Squints at her, types.*) 26.
GALLAGHER. Right, Loot. It came in too late. Night court. Right, Chief. (*Hangs up, takes other receiver.*) Sorry, Mrs. . . . (*Glances at his pad.*) Andrews? Yes. Have you a list of just what's missing? It would help. Any cash? You do? One of the servants? All right. I'll be there. Yes, madam. (*Hangs up, makes notes on scratch pad.*)
SHOPLIFTER. My God, the times I spent twice as much for a pocketbook!
DAKIS. Well, you took it.
SHOPLIFTER. I don't know why. It was crazy.
DAKIS. It's your first offense. You'll get off on probation.
SHOPLIFTER. I didn't need it. I didn't even like it. Crazy! (*A burst of song off-stage, an operatic aria.* SHOPLIFTER, *puzzled, looks about, looks at detectives inquisitively, but they're absorbed in their work.* PATROLMAN KEOGH *enters from hall* U.L. *singing.*)
KEOGH. (*Crosses to desk No.* 2.) Got any 61's?
GALLAGHER. You're off key today, Gus. (*Hands him several slips.* KEOGH *studies them, exits singing,* U.L.)
DAKIS. (*Rises, crosses to finger-print board, rolls ink on pad.*) Come here! (SHOPLIFTER *crosses up to* DAKIS. *He takes her hand. She stiffens.*) Take it easy, girlie. Let me do the work. You just supply the finger.
SHOPLIFTER. Ooh! !
DAKIS. This finger. Relax, now. I'm not going to hurt you. Just r . . r . . roll it. (*Presses her finger down on sheet.*)
GALLAGHER. (*Rises, crosses* U. C. *Glances up, toward door* U. L. *into hallway* L.) Uh-uh! Here comes trouble. Look at the calendar.
DAKIS. Full moon tonight.
GALLAGHER. It never fails.
MRS. FARRAGUT. Officer, Officer!
GALLAGHER. (*Crossing down to Desk No.* 2, *sits.*) Come in, Mrs. Farragut. Are those people still bothering you?
MRS. FARRAGUT. (*Enters* U.L., *goes to Desk No.* 2.) Worse than ever, Officer. If I hadn't wakened last night and smelled that gas coming through the walls . . . I'd be gone—we'd all be gone.
GALLAGHER. Have a chair.
MRS. FARRAGUT. Why haven't you given me protection? I demand protection.

GALLAGHER. I got twelve men on duty day and night guarding you.

MRS. FARRAGUT. But whose side are they really on? Are you sure you can trust them?

GALLAGHER. One of them is my own brother, Mrs. Farragut.

MRS. FARRAGUT. (*Sits chair* L. *of desk No.* 2.) Oh, I'm sorry! I didn't mean to offend you. Only it's so important. You see, they know I know all about it—Atom bombs. They're making them—these foreigners next door. They blow this atomic vapor through the wall at me. And they have a man watching me from the top of the Empire State Building . . . with radar . . .

GALLAGHER. We got that man covered.

MRS. FARRAGUT. You have?

GALLAGHER. Day and night.

MRS. FARRAGUT. Does the President know about this?

GALLAGHER. I talked to him only an hour ago.

MRS. FARRAGUT. Oh, that's very important. Very important. You see these foreigners know I have electronic vision. I can see everything around us vibrating with electricity . . . billions of atoms . . . stars in the universe . . . turning . . . turning . . . vibrating . . . vibrating . . . with electricity. Every human being is a dynamo. Out there in the street . . . ten million living dynamos—coming, going . . . cross-currents. (JOE FEINSON *enters from hall* U. L.) And those great tall skyscrapers draw up all this human electricity to the top of the Empire State Building, where that man sits, and he turns it back and shoots it down on us . . . it's a terrifying situation . . . terrifying.

GALLAGHER. (*Rises, crosses to her.*) Mrs. Farragut, I'm watching it . . . every second, every second. (*Takes her up to gate.*) I've got it all under control. I'm going to double the men I've got guarding you. 25 men day and night. How's that?

MRS. FARRAGUT. Oh, much better. Much better. Thank you. Thank you. (*Exits into hall* U. L.)

GALLAGHER. (*At gate of rail* U. L.) Get out the butterfly net.

JOE. You sure do a good hand job.

GALLAGHER. (*Crossing down to desk No.* 2, *sits.*) This job is ninety per cent salesmanship!

DAKIS. (*Finishes fingerprinting.*) O. K., girlie, wash your hands. In there! (*Points to washroom door up* R., *and sits desk No.* 1. SHOPLIFTER *crosses to washroom.*)

JOE. (*Crossing down to desk No. 2.*) What's new?

GALLAGHER. It's quiet. (*Knocks wood.*)

JOE. The town's dead as Kelcey's. (*Saunters over to* GALLAGHER'S *desk, sits* L. *of desk No. 2.*)

SHOPLIFTER. There isn't any lock on the door. (*Opens washroom door, frowning.*)

DAKIS. Just wash your hands.

SHOPLIFTER. Fine thing! (*Slams door.*)

JOE. Story for me?

GALLAGHER. No. Shoplifter.

JOE. She anybody?

GALLAGHER. Nobody at all.

JOE. Any angles?

GALLAGHER. Nah! Just a slob. (TWO DETECTIVES *enter from hall* U. L., *both youngish men. One of them,* CALLAHAN, *is very exuberant and high-spirited, Tenth Avenue in his speech, dressed in a flashy yellow shirt and baggy trousers, which do not match his wrinkled jacket. The other,* DETECTIVE O'BRIEN, *is an older man, neatly dressed, soft-spoken.*)

CALLAHAN. (*Off-stage.*) Come on, Johnny, my feet are killing me. (*Enters, crosses between desk No. 1 and No. 2.*) Hi, Tom, Nick, Joe! Gee, it's hot out. Sweat your kolonjas off!

JOE. What the hell are you dressed up for? Must be Hallowe'en?

CALLAHAN. Wonder what he means?

O'BRIEN. Saks-Fifth Avenue pays Mike to advertise their clothes.

CALLAHAN. Boy, were we given the runaround! We tailed a guy for two hours, from fifty-thoird to 91st and back. Looked like a good man, didn't he? (*Crosses to files* U. R.)

O'BRIEN. Sure did.

CALLAHAN. Then the jerko took a bus. (*Looks at his schedule.*) Moider! Sunday again! What the hell am I? A Sunday detective? My kids'll grow up and they won't even know me. (*Crosses to* JOE.) Say, Joe, there's a big story on Thoird Avenue. You get it? The brewery truck?

JOE. No, what about it?

CALLAHAN. A brewery truck backed up into the sidewalk and a barrel of beer fell right into a baby carriage.

JOE. Was the baby in it?

CALLAHAN. Yeah.

JOE. Was it killed?

CALLAHAN. No, it was light beer! Ha! Ha! Ha! (*Crosses to gate up* C.)

JOE. (*Groans.*) You're a cute kid. What's your name, Berle? (SHOPLIFTER *comes from washroom and crosses to desk No. 1.* DAKIS *says* " *Sit down.*" SHOPLIFTER *sits above desk No. 1.*)

O'BRIEN. (*Crossing down to desk No.* 2.) Busy day?

GALLAGHER. Quiet.

O'BRIEN. Good. (*Knocks wood.*)

GALLAGHER. Too quiet.

O'BRIEN. We're due. We're ripe for a homicide.

GALLAGHER. Ssh! Wait till I get out of here. (*Desk phone rings,* GALLAGHER *groans.*) Can't you keep your big mouth shut? (O'BRIEN *crosses to table* U. C. *Picks up receiver.*) 21st Squad Detectives, Gallagher. Yes, Madam. What is it you lost?

JOE. Her virginity.

GALLAGHER. In a taxicab?

JOE. Hell of a place!

GALLAGHER. Did you get his number? Can you describe it?

JOE. This is going to be very educational.

GALLAGHER. What's your name? Address? Yes, Madam. I'll check that for you. Not at all.

JOE. (*Simultaneously with* GALLAGHER'S *last speech.*) I got a squeal for you. I lost something. My manhood.

CALLAHAN. (*Crossing to* JOE *up to file,* U. L., *files card, then to table.*) We don't take cases *that* old, Joe. (JOE *crosses to* CALLAHAN.)

GALLAGHER. (*Hanging up.*) Outlawed by the statute of limitations. (DETECTIVE LOU BRODY *enters* U. L. *with several containers of coffee, and a bag of sandwiches. Crosses to desk No. 1, table and* LIEUTENANT'S *office to leave coat and hat on hatrack.*)

BRODY. Here you are, Nick!

DAKIS. Thanks, Lou, I appreciate that.

BRODY. My pleasure. Here you are, Miss.

SHOPLIFTER. With Russian Dressing? (*Standing up, searching in purse.*)

BRODY. (*Enters* LIEUTENANT'S *office* R., *hangs hat and coat on hat-tree.*) They ran out.

SHOPLIFTER. How much do I owe you?

DAKIS. It's on the house.

SHOPLIFTER. You're all awful decent. You know, really, awful decent.
DAKIS. Well, you didn't kill anyone. (*A middle-aged man,* SIMS, *enters from hall* U. L., *well-dressed, carrying a briefcase. He appears at railing* U. L.)
GALLAGHER. Yes, sir? (SIMS *fishes a card out of his wallet and presents it.*)
SIMS. My name is Sims, Endicott Sims. I'm an attorney.
GALLAGHER. What can we do for you, Counsellor?
SIMS. (*Crossing to desk No.* 2.) I represent Mr. Kurt Schneider. Your office has a warrant out for him?
DAKIS. Hey, Lou! This is Jim's squeal, ain't it? Kurt Schneider?
BRODY. Yeah. I'll take it. (*Crosses to* SIMS U. C.) This is my partner's case. What about Schneider, Counsellor? Where is he?
SIMS. He's ready to surrender himself into your custody.
BRODY. Fine, bring him in.
SIMS. First, however, I have here some photographs. . . . (*Takes photos from his briefcase, hands them to* BRODY.) He had these taken half an hour ago.
BRODY. Naked? Ugly, ain't he?
SIMS. He's no Mr. America.
BRODY. No, that he ain't.
SIMS. The purpose is not esthetic. I don't want any rubber hoses used on him.
BRODY. Counsellor, how long have you been practicing law? We don't assault our prisoners.
SIMS. Who's handling this case here?
BRODY. My partner.
SIMS. A man named James McLeod?
BRODY. Yeah.
SIMS. I've heard a good deal about him. A law unto himself. You will please tell him for me. . . . (MCLEOD *is heard off-stage. Ad lib.* CALLAHAN *goes into* LIEUTENANT'S *office.*)
BRODY. Wait a minute. Tell him for yourself. Here he is. (JAMES MCLEOD *comes from hall into the room, leading by the arm* ARTHUR KINDRED, *a young man with a sensitive face.*) Oh, Jim, this is your squeal. (*To* SIMS.) Detective McLeod . . . Mr. Sims.
MCLEOD. How do you do, sir?
SIMS. How do you do?
BRODY. Mr. Sims is an attorney.

MCLEOD. And very clever. I've seen him in court.
SIMS. Thank you.
BRODY. He's here for Kurt Schneider.
MCLEOD. Oh, yes. (*To* SIMS.) I had the pleasure of arresting your client a year ago.
SIMS. So I am informed.
MCLEOD. He's changed his lawyer since, if not his business.
SIMS. Kurt Schneider is a successful truck farmer from New Jersey.
MCLEOD. With a little abortion mill in New York for a sideline. Nothing fancy, just a quick-ice-tong job. (*Throws hat on table* U. C.) I've a yen for your client.
SIMS. I'm aware of that. (*Takes pictures from* BRODY *and hands them to* MCLEOD.) Take a look at these pictures.
MCLEOD. (*Looks at pictures, grimaces.*) There's no doubt the process of evolution is now reversing itself.
SIMS. You understand, officer, that my client has certain rights. I don't want to be antagonistic, but I am here to defend my client.
MCLEOD. One second, Counsellor. I'll be right with you. Have a chair. (O'BRIEN *pushes one of chairs below table to* L. *of table.* SIMS *sits.* MCLEOD *guides the young man into the squad room to below desk No.* 2 *toward bench* D. R.)
GALLAGHER. Jim, call your wife!
MCLEOD. Thanks, Tom. When'd she phone? (*Phone buzzer sounds, desk No.* 2 *phone. Crosses* D. R. *with* ARTHUR.)
GALLAGHER. Twenty minutes ago.
MCLEOD. All right, Buster. Sit down over there. (ARTHUR *sits bench* R.)
GALLAGHER. 21st Squad Detectives, Gallagher. Yes, sir. Oh, Jim, the Lieutenant. (*Hands phone to* MCLEOD.)
MCLEOD. (*Takes phone and it is evident from the faces he makes that he has no great love for his Lieutenant. Sits on desk No.* 2.) Yes, Lieutenant, I just got back.
JOE. (*Crosses down, pulls chair with him, sits on chair next to* MCLEOD.) Hi'ya, Seamus.
MCLEOD. (*Smothers mouthpiece of phone.*) Oh, Yussel, Yussel! You're supposed to be an intelligent reporter.
JOE. What's the matter, Seamus?
MCLEOD. That Langdon story!
JOE. Didn't I spell your name right?

MCLEOD. It's the only thing you did get right. (*On phone.*) Yes, Lieutenant. I just brought him in. (*To* ARTHUR.) Arthur, were you arrested before?

ARTHUR. I told you.

MCLEOD. Tell me again.

ARTHUR. No.

MCLEOD. (*Back to phone.*) Says no. We'll check his prints. Yes, sir. Yes, sir. (*Covers mouthpiece.*) You're degenerating into a real sob-sister, Yussel. Grrrim grray prrrison walls! Wish you'd have seen Langdon in the bullpen. "Hiya, Jack! Hiya, Charley!" Smiling. He was happy! He was home again! (*On phone.*) Yes, Lieutenant. Yes, sir.

JOE. The mortal God—McLeod! Captain Ahab pursuing the great gray Leviathan! A fox with rabies bit him in the ass when he was two years old, and neither of them recovered. Don't throw water on McLeod. He goes rabid!

MCLEOD. (*Hangs up.*) You apple-headed member of the Fourth Estate—to look natural, you should have a knife and fork sticking out of the top of your head. City College is going to be proud of you yet! (*Rises, starts towards* LIEUTENANT'S *door* R. *Turns back to* JOE, *talks Jewish.*) Mir daft ihr dihagginun!

JOE. (*Still seated—pushing chair to* U. L. *of desk No.* 2.) Is this story worth a picture?

MCLEOD. Later, Joe! . . . Later. (*To* ARTHUR.) Don't try running for it, Buster. You'd just about reach that door and suddenly you'd put on weight. Bullets are supersonic.

ARTHUR. Don't worry. (BRODY *crosses* D. *below desk No.* 2 *to* ARTHUR.)

MCLEOD. I won't. Either way. (BRODY *comes over, scrutinizes* ARTHUR'S *face.*) Know him?

BRODY. No. . . . No . . . I . . . (*Shakes head.*)

MCLEOD. (*Calls across the room to* SIMS.) One second, Counsellor. (*Crosses to* LIEUTENANT'S *office, comes face to face with* CALLAHAN. *Pauses to survey* CALLAHAN'S *attire. Shakes his head.*) Strictly Pier 6!

CALLAHAN. I ain't no friggin barber-college detective with a Brooks Brothers coat. (*Crosses to files, takes out card, crosses up to table* U. C.)

MCLEOD. No, you *ain't*. . . . (*Goes into* LIEUTENANT'S *office, dials a number on* LIEUTENANT'S *phone.*)

CALLAHAN. (*Miffed.*) Remind me to get that college graduate a bicycle pump for Christmas to blow up that big head of his.
O'BRIEN. He needling you again?
CALLAHAN. Yeah! Big needle-man from sew-and-sew. (*Laughs at his own joke.* JOE *rises—joins* CALLAHAN *at table* U. C.)
MCLEOD. (*Sits on desk No.* 3.) Hello! Hello, darling. (*His voice at once takes on warmth and tenderness, his eyes, his smile, his whole being seem to undergo a metamorphosis.*) What did the doctor say? Yeah! Good! Good! Mm. Nothing organic? Sure? Sure, now, Mary. How does he explain those palpitations? Psychosomatic? Mm! And how does he explain that? Yeah! What tensions? (*Laughs.*) What'd he prescribe . . . short of a new world? Mm, h'm! Phenobarbital and Vitamin B-one. The history of our times. (*Laughs.*) Oh, Mary! You're wonderful. I love you. . . . I'll call you later, darling. Good-bye. (*In squad room,* ARTHUR *goes a greenish color, clutches his stomach and bites his lip.* BRODY, *who has been studying him, crosses to him.*)
BRODY. What's the matter, sonny?
ARTHUR. Nothing.
BRODY. Would you like a drink of whisky?
ARTHUR. No, thanks.
BRODY. In there. (BRODY *points to washroom* U. R. ARTHUR *goes in. Desk phone rings, desk No.* 2. GALLAGHER *reaches for it.*) O. K., Tom. I'll take over now. Go on home. (*Picks up phone.*)
GALLAGHER. Home? I got a squeal. (GALLAGHER *takes coat from back of chair and exits door* R., LIEUTENANT'S *office.*)
BRODY. (*On phone. Sits at desk No.* 2.) 21st Squad. Detective Brody. Yeah? Get his license number? . . . (*Glances at clock, scribbles data on pad.*)
MCLEOD. (*Enters squad room from* LIEUTENANT'S *office, crosses to* SIMS U. L.) Now, Counsellor?
SIMS. (*Rises. Presents him with the photos again.*) You will observe there are no scars or lacerations of any kind! (*Points to photos.*) This is the way I'm delivering my client to you, and this is the way I want him back.
MCLEOD. I should think that any change whatsoever would be an improvement, Counsellor.
SIMS. I want you to know I'm not going to allow you to violate his Constitutional rights. You're not going to abuse him physically or degrade his dignity as a human being—understand?

MCLEOD. (*Bites this off.*) Counsellor, I never met a criminal yet who didn't wrap himself in the Constitution from head to toe—or a hoodlum that wasn't filled to the nostrils with habeas corpus and the rights of human dignity. Did you ever see the girl your client operated on last year—in the morgue—on a marble slab? Wasn't much human left of her, Counsellor—and very little dignity ——

SIMS. My client was innocent of that charge. The court acquitted him.

MCLEOD. He was guilty.

SIMS. Are you setting yourself above the courts of the land?

MCLEOD. There's a higher court, Counsellor. . . .

SIMS. I'm sure there is, Officer. Are you qualified to speak for it? I'm not. I'm not one of the elite. God doesn't come down and whisper in my ear, but it comes to the man-made law on terra firma, I know it, I obey it, and I respect it.

MCLEOD. What do you want to do? Try the case here? This isn't a court of law. Save it for the Judge. Now . . . Counsellor—we're busy here. You'll excuse me, I'm certain. Your client will be treated with as much delicacy as he is entitled to. So bring him in—or get off the pot. (*Crosses to desk No.* 2.)

SIMS. I've heard about you. You're quite an anomaly, McLeod. Quite an anomaly. . . . It's going to be a real pleasure to examine you on the witness stand.

MCLEOD. Anything to give you a thrill, Counsellor. (*Throws photos on desk No.* 2.)

SIMS. We may have a thriller or two in store for you.

MCLEOD. Meaning?

SIMS. For over a year you have been personally making my client's life a living hell. Why?

MCLEOD. I beg your pardon.

SIMS. Why?

MCLEOD. (*Crossing to* SIMS. ARTHUR *exits from washroom and stands by file cabinet* U. R.) Because I'm annoyed by criminals that get away with murder. They upset me.

SIMS. You're easily upset.

MCLEOD. I'm very sensitive. To me your client is just another criminal. (*Turns away, dismissing* SIMS.) O. K., Arthur. In there. (*Pointing to* LIEUTENANT'S *office.* ARTHUR *enters* LIEUTENANT'S *office.*)

SIMS. That's your story. At considerable expense we have investigated and discovered otherwise. (*Exit into hall* U. L.)
BRODY. What the hell's he driving at?
MCLEOD. A fishing expedition. That's a shrewd mouthpiece. I've seen him operate. (*Goes into* LIEUTENANT'S *office. Speaks to* ARTHUR.) Take everything out of your pockets and put them on the desk. (ARTHUR *takes contents of his pockets with* MCLEOD'S *help and places them on desk.*) That all?
ARTHUR. Yes.
MCLEOD. (*Upstage of desk No.* 3.) Turn your pockets inside out. (ARTHUR *obeys.*) Sit down over there. What'd you do with the money?
ARTHUR. (*Sits chair* D. L. *in* LIEUTENANT'S *office.*) I spent it.
MCLEOD. (*Examines articles one by one, very carefully.*) All of it?
ARTHUR. Yes.
MCLEOD. (*Picks up book of Stork Club matches.*) When were you at the Stork Club?
ARTHUR. Wednesday night.
MCLEOD. Been doing the hot spots?
ARTHUR. Some.
MCLEOD. Any of the money left?
ARTHUR. How far can you go with four hundred dollars?
MCLEOD. Four hundred and eighty.
ARTHUR. Was it four-eighty?
MCLEOD. So your employer claims.
ARTHUR. He ought to know.
MCLEOD. Arthur, why'd you take the money?
ARTHUR. What's the difference? I took it, I admit it, I took it!
MCLEOD. Where'd you spend last night?
ARTHUR. In my room.
MCLEOD. I was there. Where were you? Under the bed?
ARTHUR. I sat in the Park.
MCLEOD. (*Crossing* D. *to* ARTHUR.) All night?
ARTHUR. Yes.
MCLEOD. (*Moving down.*) It rained.
ARTHUR. Drizzled.
MCLEOD. You sat in the drizzle?
ARTHUR. Yes.
MCLEOD. What were you doing?
ARTHUR. Just dreaming.

MCLEOD. In the park at night? Dreaming?

ARTHUR. Night is a time for dreams.

MCLEOD. (*Crossing to desk No. 3.*) And *thieves!* (MCLEOD *examines the articles. Phone buzzer in squad room, desk No. 2, sounds.* BRODY *answers.*)

BRODY. 21st Squad. Detective Brody. Callahan, for you.

CALLAHAN. (*Crosses, lays parking ticket on desk No. 2.*) A kiss from Judge Bromfield. (*Into phone.*) Callahan!

JOE. (*Crossing* D. *to desk No. 2. Examines ticket.*) You get a parking ticket?

DAKIS. (*Morosely.*) I got one, too. In front of the Criminal Court Building. You're such a big shot, Joe. Why don't you do something about it?

JOE. (*To* BRODY.) Mind if I use the phone?

BRODY. Go ahead. The outside one. (JOE *takes up phone at* U. *corner desk No. 2 and dials a number.*)

O'BRIEN. (*Crossing to behind* JOE *to gate,* U. L.) Some of these judges haven't the brains God gave them. They refrigerate them in law school.

DAKIS. It isn't enough we use our own cars to take our prisoners to court. We got to use our own gas. We can't even deduct it from our income tax. How do you like that!

JOE. (*Into phone.*) Hello, Jerry—this is Joe Feinson. (*Screaming.*) Who the hell does that Judge Bromfield think he is? He's persecutin' cops, that's what. Parkin' tickets on duty. Yeah! I'm going to stir up a hornets' nest. All right! All right! (*Calmly.*) Yeah. Fine. Sure. I got one here. All right. Yeah. Fine. (*Hangs up, takes ticket.*) O. K. Forget it. It's fixed. (*Crosses to get* DAKIS' *ticket on desk No. 1.*)

O'BRIEN. You frighten him?

JOE. I frightened myself. Look at my hand shaking. (DAKIS *laughs heartily.*)

CALLAHAN. A cop's got to get a reporter to fix a ticket for him! Now I've seen everything.

JOE. (*Crossing to* CALLAHAN.) That's the way it should be. A free press is the tocsin of a free people. The law keeps you in line, we keep the law in line, the people keep *us* in line, you keep the people in line. Everybody kicks everybody else in the ass! That way nobody gets too big for his britches. That's democracy! (*Crosses to* U. L. *gate.*)

DAKIS. You have the gall to call that yellow, monopolistic sheet—a free press? Ha! Ha! You kill me. (*Exit* JOE *through door in wall* U. L., *waving ticket.*)
SHOPLIFTER. (*Rises.*) So?
DAKIS. So . . . what?
SHOPLIFTER. So what happens to me now?
DAKIS. We wait here till night court opens. Nine o'clock. Then the magistrate will probably set bail for you.
O'BRIEN. (*Crossing to* SHOPLIFTER.) Have you got a lawyer? You might save the bail bond.
SHOPLIFTER. My brother-in-law's a lawyer.
DAKIS. (*Belches.*) Excuse me! Call him up. . . .
SHOPLIFTER. Gee, I hate to. He's kind of a new brother-in-law. If my sister finds out . . . Oh, God! She'll die . . . and she's in the fourth month, too.
O'BRIEN. (*Crossing* D. L. *to files.*) It's up to you.
DAKIS. Suit yourself. . . . The court'll appoint you one.
SHOPLIFTER. (*Sits.*) Gee, I don't know what to do. . . .
MCLEOD. Ever been arrested before, Arthur?
ARTHUR. I told you no.
MCLEOD. You sure?
ARTHUR. Yes.
MCLEOD. It would help your case if you returned the money.
ARTHUR. I know. But I can't. I told you it's gone. (BRODY *rises from desk No. 2, enters Lieutenant's office and listens to interrogation. Leans against door jamb.*)
MCLEOD. What's this pawn ticket for?
ARTHUR. Text books.
MCLEOD. Where did you get them?
ARTHUR. College.
MCLEOD. Graduate?
ARTHUR. No.
MCLEOD. What stopped you?
ARTHUR. World War Two, the first time.
MCLEOD. And the second time?
ARTHUR. World War Three.
MCLEOD. Foolish question, foolish answer. (*Examining contents of* ARTHUR'S *pockets.*) Have you any identifying marks on you, Arthur? Any scars? . . . Roll up your sleeves. . . . (ARTHUR *obeys. On his* L. *wrist is a tattoo mark.*) A tattoo mark. A heart.

And what's the name? (*Crosses to* ARTHUR.) J—O—Y! Who's Joy?

ARTHUR. A girl.

MCLEOD. Your girl?

ARTHUR. No.

MCLEOD. (*Sits swivel chair.*) Whose girl?

ARTHUR. What's the difference?

MCLEOD. What branch of the service were you in?

ARTHUR. Navy.

MCLEOD. How long?

ARTHUR. Five years.

MCLEOD. What rank?

ARTHUR. Chief Petty Officer.

MCLEOD. You married?

ARTHUR. No.

MCLEOD. How old are you?

ARTHUR. Twenty-seven.

MCLEOD. How long you been in New York?

ARTHUR. A year.

MCLEOD. Where you from?

ARTHUR. Ann Arbor, Michigan. (BRODY *crosses to back of desk No. 3.*)

MCLEOD. What's your father's business?

ARTHUR. My father's dead.

MCLEOD. What *was* his business?

ARTHUR. He was a teacher. Music. History of music.

MCLEOD. History of music? Where's your mother?

ARTHUR. She's dead.

MCLEOD. (*Looking through* ARTHUR'S *address book.*) Ah! Here's Joy again—Joy Carmichael. Maybe I better give her a ring?

ARTHUR. What for? Why drag her into this? She doesn't know anything about it.

MCLEOD. (*Mockingly.*) You wouldn't lie to me, would you, Arthur?

ARTHUR. Why should I lie?

MCLEOD. I don't know. Why should you steal? Maybe it's because you're just no damn good, hm, Arthur? The judge asks me, I'm going to throw the book at you.—Tattoo that on your arm! (MCLEOD *rises.*)

BRODY. Admission?

MCLEOD. Yes.

BRODY. Got the money?

MCLEOD. No. He doesn't milk easily. A superman. I've got an angle. (*Crosses into the squad room, sits at desk No. 2, dials phone.*)

BRODY. (*Crossing* D. *to* ARTHUR.) Sonny, you look like a nice boy. How'd you get into this mess?

ARTHUR. (*Rises.*) What is this? Are you going to give me a lecture?

BRODY. Don't get funny with me, son. I'll knock you right through the floor! Sit down! (ARTHUR *sits.*) How'd you get into this mess, son? (BRODY *sits chair* L. *of desk.*)

ARTHUR. I don't know. You get trapped.

BRODY. Where's the money?

ARTHUR. (*Shakes head.*) Gone! It's gone.

BRODY. What did you do with it?

ARTHUR. Spent it.

BRODY. (*Pauses, takes out cigarette, offers* ARTHUR *one, lights both.*) You went to college? What did you study?

ARTHUR. Majored in History.

BRODY. History? What for?

ARTHUR. To teach. I wanted to be a teacher.

BRODY. Much of a career in that?

ARTHUR. I used to think so.

BRODY. You're a long way from home?

ARTHUR. Yes.

BRODY. Why didn't you finish?

ARTHUR. No time. There's no time. You can't start from scratch at twenty-five. (*Loud voices off-stage.*)

CALLAHAN. (*Rises from chair at* U. C. *table.*) Uh-uh! Here comes trouble! A couple of customers. (*Crosses* D. *to desk No.* 2. PATROLMAN BARNES *enters* U. L. *with* TWO BURGLARS, LEWIS *and* CHARLIE, *handcuffed to each other . . . followed by a hysterical* MRS. BAGATELLE *and* JANITOR. BRODY, *hearing the noise, crosses back into squad room to* D. R. DAKIS *rises.*)

MCLEOD. (*Rises.*) What have you got there?

PATROLMAN BARNES. (*A Negro.* L. *of desk No.* 2.) Burglars. Caught 'em red-handed. Forcible entry.

MRS. BAGATELLE. (R. *of desk No. 1. In French accent.*) I come up to my apartment. The door was open. The lock was burst wide open. The jamb was broken down. They were inside. I started to run. This one grabbed me and choked me.

1ST BURGLAR (CHARLIE). It's a lie! It's a pack of lies! I don't know what she's talking about. . . .

BARNES. I was right across the street when I heard her scream. They come running down the stairs. I collared them. . . . This one put up a struggle.

CHARLIE. (*Screaming across desk at* MCLEOD.) I was walkin' down the stairs mindin' my own business—the cop jumps on me and starts beatin' the crap outa me.

MCLEOD. (*Crossing around back of desk No. 2 to* LEWIS. *Gruffly.*) All right! We'll come to you.

CHARLIE. Think I'm crazy to do a thing like this?

BRODY. (*Crossing to chair below desk No. 2, moves it* D. S. *for* CHARLIE.) You'll get your turn to talk. Sit down.

BARNES. On this one I found a jimmy, and this. . . . (*Takes out revolver from his own pocket, hands it to* MCLEOD.)

BRODY. Twenty-two?

MCLEOD. Yeah, loaded.

BRODY. (*To* CHARLIE.) What's your name? Stand up! (*Searches him more thoroughly.*)

CHARLIE. Gennini. Charles Gennini. And I don't know nothin'. I don't even know this guy. (*To* LEWIS.) Ask him! Do I know you? No!

BRODY. Take it easy, Charlie. Sit down! (CHARLIE *sits. Crosses to* LEWIS.) What's your name?

LEWIS. Lewis Abbott.

BRODY. (*Brandishes revolver and jimmy.*) Were you carrying these, Lewis?

LEWIS. (*Matter-of-fact.*) Ya.

MRS. BAGATELLE. (*Crosses* D. S. *Begins to cry.*) By the throat he grabbed me! How can this happen in New York?

MCLEOD. (*Gently. Places chair* R. *of desk No. 1 for her.*) Take it easy, madam. You're all right, now. Sit down. I'll get you a nice cold glass of water. (*She sits.*)

MRS. BAGATELLE. Oh, please, please! (MCLEOD *crosses into washroom* U. R.)

BRODY. You're a bad boy, Lewis, and what's more, you're a bad thief. Don't you know a good thief never carries a loaded pistol? It means five years added to your sentence, Lewis.

LEWIS. I'd never use it.

BRODY. That's what you think, Lewis. But it'd happen. You're lucky you were picked up. Probably saved you from a murder rap. Just once you'd walk in—a woman, she'd scream, resist, you'd get scared . . .

CALLAHAN. (*Crossing to* D. R. *of desk No.* 2.) Boom! Boom! (*Sings a funeral dirge.*) Ta da de da da de da de da de dum. . . .

BRODY. You like the smell of burning flesh? Your own?

LEWIS. Na. (MCLEOD *returns from washroom with glass of water, gives it to* MRS. BAGATELLE.)

BRODY. Getting dropped today was the luckiest thing ever happened to you. (*Turns to* CHARLIE. *Pulls him to his feet.*) Now, *you!* (CHARLIE *rises.* BRODY *searches him more carefully.*)

CHARLIE. I got nothing to do with this, I swear. You think' I got rocks in my head?

BRODY. (*Producing a large wad of bills from* CHARLIE'S *pockets.*) Look at this!

MCLEOD. (*Takes roll from* BRODY.) Quite a bundle! How much is here, Charlie?

CHARLIE. Fourteen hundred bucks.

MCLEOD. (*Crosses to* CHARLIE. *Digs into his own pocket, takes out tiny roll of bills.*) Eleven! Why is it every time one of you bums comes in, you've got fourteen hundred dollars in your kick, and I've got eleven in mine?

BRODY. You don't live right.

MCLEOD. No, evidently not. (*To* CHARLIE.) Where'd you get this?

CHARLIE. I saved it. I worked.

MCLEOD. Where?

CHARLIE. I was a bricklayer.

MCLEOD. (*Hands money to* BARNES, *who crosses to desk, counts money.*) Count this. This goes to the custodian. (*To* CHARLIE.) Let's see your hands! (*He feels them.*) The only thing you ever laid, Charlie, was a two-dollar floozy. (DAKIS *sits at desk No. 1. Gives* BARNES *envelope for money.*)

CALLAHAN. (*Down to* CHARLIE.) Do you always carry so much money around?

CHARLIE. Yeah.

MCLEOD. What's the matter, Charlie . . . don't you trust the banks?

BRODY. (*Crosses to back of* D. C. *chair.*) When were you in stir last, Charlie?
CHARLIE. Me? In jail? Never. I swear to God on a stack of Bibles.
MCLEOD. What's your B number?
CHARLIE. I ain't got none.
MCLEOD. You sure?
CHARLIE. On my mother's grave! I ain't got no B card.
CALLAHAN. You're stupid.
MCLEOD. You just gave yourself away, Charlie. . . . How do you know what a B card is . . . if you never had one?
CHARLIE. I . . . I . . . heard . . . I been around.
MCLEOD. I'll bet you have. You've been working this precinct for the last three months.
CHARLIE. No. I swear . . .
MCLEOD. (*Laughs in his face.*) Who the hell do you think you're kidding? (CHARLIE *glares at him.*) I know that face. This is a good man. He's been in jail before.
CHARLIE. Never. So help me, God! What are you tryin' to do? Hang me? I wanta call my lawyer. (*Tries to reach for phone on desk No. 2, stopped by* BRODY *and* CALLAHAN *standing back of him.*)
MCLEOD. Shut up! Print him. You'll find he's got a sheet as long as your arm.
CHARLIE. I don't know what you're talkin' about. I swear to God! I get down on my knees . . . (*Falls to his knees, crying.*) What do you want me to . . . ?
MCLEOD. Get up! Get up! I can smell you. He's a cat burglar. A real murderer!
CALLAHAN. (*Turns* U. S.) How many women you raped? (CALLAHAN *stands nearby, his back to prisoner, his revolver sticking out of holster.* CHARLIE *looks at it. As he moves fast to bench* R. *sits.*)
MCLEOD. (*To* CALLAHAN.) Watch the roscoe! (CALLAHAN *takes his revolver out of his holster, puts it in pocket.*)
MRS. BAGATELLE. Isn't anybody going to take care of me?
MCLEOD. (*Crossing to woman, seated* L.) Look, madam! You're very upset. We don't need you here. Why don't you go home and rest up?
MRS. BAGATELLE. No, no, no! I am afraid to go back there now. I'm afraid even to go out in the street.

MCLEOD. (*Laughs.*) Now come on. You've got nothing to be afraid of. Suppose I send a policeman with you? What time do you expect your husband back?

MRS. BAGATELLE. Seven o'clock.

MCLEOD. I'll send a policeman home with you to keep you company. A nice handsome Irish cop. How's that?

MRS. BAGATELLE. (*Thinks it over, giggles at him, nods.*) That would be fine. Thank you very much!

MCLEOD. (*Turns her over to* KEOGH, D. *stage of gate* U. L.) Gus, see that this lady gets home safely. (PATROLMAN KEOGH *takes her in tow. Exit* KEOGH *and* MRS. BAGATELLE, *giggling, by hall* U. L.)

BRODY. (MCLEOD *calls* O'BRIEN, *crosses to* LEWIS, *who sits.*) Now, Lewis, sit down. You're in trouble. (*Placing chair* L. *of desk No.* 2.)

SHOPLIFTER. (*Sitting chair above desk No.* 1.) I think I better call my brother-in-law.

DAKIS. What's the number?

SHOPLIFTER. Jerome 7-2577. (DAKIS *crosses to phone on desk No.* 2, *dials number.*)

MCLEOD. You help us, we'll help you. We'll ask the D. A. to give you a break.

BRODY. Tell us the truth. How many burglaries you committed here? (LEWIS *is silent.*)

CALLAHAN. Be a man! You got dropped! Face it!

O'BRIEN. Why not get the agony over with?

CALLAHAN. If you don't—we gonna get the D. A. to throw away the key. (MCLEOD *and* BRODY *go to* LIEUTENANT'S *office files.* CALLAHAN *sits* U. S. *end desk No.* 2. O'BRIEN *at* U. C. *window.*)

DAKIS. (*To* SHOPLIFTER.) All right. Here you are, girlie. Come and get it. (*Hands her phone* L. *stage end desk No.* 2.)

SHOPLIFTER. (*Stands* D. L. *end desk No.* 2.) Oh, God! What'll I tell her? What should I say? (*Crosses to phone, takes it and assumes casual voice.*) Oh, hello, Milly. Yeah. . . . Nothin'! I just didn't have any change. How are you? . . . Fine. . . . How was the party? You went to Brooklyn? In your delicate condition? Milly! Yeah. . . . Yeah. (*Laughs feebly.*) Oh! What do you know? Say, Milly . . . is . . . er . . . is . . . Jack there by any chance? Could I talk to him? Oh, nothin'! Some friend of mine wants some advice . . . on somethin'! . . . I don't know. . . . (*Puts hand over mouthpiece.*) He's there . . . what should

I tell him? I don't know what to tell him. . . . (SIMS *appears with* KURT SCHNEIDER *at gate* U. L. *Ad lib. with* BARNES *at rail.*)

DAKIS. Tell him to meet you at night court, 101 Center Street. . . .

SHOPLIFTER. Shall I tell him to bring hard cash?

DAKIS. He'll know better than we . . .

SHOPLIFTER. (*Her voice changes.*) Hello, Jack? Listen—can Milly hear me? I don't want her to know, but I'm in a jam. I need your help. So don't let on. Make out like it's nothing. I can't give you all the details. I'm at the police station. Yeah. . . . I took a bag. . . . Best's. I had to admit it, Jack. . . . It was on my arm. Thanks, Jack. 101 Center Street. If Milly asks, tell her . . . Gee, Jack . . . you're a . . . prince with a capital "P." (*Hangs up slowly, sighs with relief to detective.*) Boy! Am I relieved!

DAKIS. Sit down there. (*He and* SHOPLIFTER *cross up to table* U. C. *She sits chair* R. *end of table.* MCLEOD *comes out of* LIEUTENANT'S *office, on* SHOPLIFTER'S *cue: "—101 Center Street." Crosses to* U. C. *desk and takes container of coffee and empty container. Turns and sees* KURT *and* SIMS *standing by gate.*)

MCLEOD. Hello, Kurt! Come on in. (*Crosses to* SIMS.)

SIMS. (*To* MCLEOD.) I have advised my client of his legal rights. He will answer no questions other than his name and address. Remember, Kurt! Name and address, that's all. Is that understood?

MCLEOD. As you say, Counsellor.

SIMS. When are you going to book him?

MCLEOD. In a couple of hours, when we get around to it.

SIMS. I want to arrange his bail bond.

MCLEOD. You'll have to get Judge Carter to stand bail for him.

SIMS. Suppose you tend to your business and I'll tend to mine!

MCLEOD. I'll be glad to, if you'll get the hell out of here and let me.

SIMS. Remember, Kurt! Name and address, that's all. (*Exits* U. L.)

MCLEOD. Sit down, Kurt. Over here! How you been? (*Crosses with* KURT *to desk No. 1, sets chair for him* D. L. *of desk.*)

KURT. So—so.

MCLEOD. You look good, Kurt. That farm life agrees with you. Some coffee?

KURT. You got enough?

MCLEOD. Sure. There's plenty. (*Pours coffee into empty container.*) Here you are! Sandwich?

KURT. I just ate.

MCLEOD. Cruller?

KURT. I'm full ——

MCLEOD. Be right with you. (*Hands him newspaper, crosses to table* U. C.)

BRODY. Steve! Take Charlie in there. (*Pointing to washroom.*)

BARNES. Come on, Charlie, in here! (*Takes* CHARLIE *off into washroom. Goes in with him, closes door.* DAKIS *enters* LIEUTENANT'S *office, gets list from files,* U. R.)

BRODY. (*Crossing to* LEWIS.) Charlie *let* you carry the gun and the jimmy. . . . You're the one that's going to burn. Don't you see how he's crossed you?

CALLAHAN. (*Crossing down, sits desk No.* 2.) You ever hear of the guy who sold his buddy up the river for thirty pieces of silver? (O'BRIEN *crosses back of* LEWIS. MCLEOD *crosses back of* LEWIS.)

LEWIS. Ya.

O'BRIEN. Well? Think!

BRODY. When were you in jail last? (*Silence.*)

MCLEOD. Look, Lewis, we're gonna fingerprint you—in half an hour we'll know your whole record, anyway.

BRODY. Make it easy for yourself. How many burglaries have you committed in New York, Lewis?

LEWIS. What'll I get?

CALLAHAN. Were you in jail before? (DAKIS *crosses out of office with list to* L. *of* BRODY.)

LEWIS. Yeah. Elmira. I got out in March.

BRODY. How long were you in?

LEWIS. Three and a half years.

BRODY. What for?

LEWIS. Burglary.

BRODY. Well—I'd say—seven and a half to 10, maybe less—if you cooperate—if not—15 to 20.

LEWIS. What do you want to know?

BRODY. How many burglaries have you committed in New York?

LEWIS. Nine or ten. . . .

CALLAHAN. That's better.

BRODY. What'd you do with the stuff?

LEWIS. Gave it to Charlie.

CALLAHAN. He was in on it, then?

LEWIS. Yes.

BRODY. He sell it?

LEWIS. Yeah.

BRODY. Where?

LEWIS. In Boston . . . I think.

BRODY. You think? Didn't he tell you?

LEWIS. No.

CALLAHAN. You're a bit of a shmuck, ain't you, Lewis?

BRODY. No, Lewis is all right. He's cooperating. How much did Charlie give you altogether?

LEWIS. Half. . . . Four hundred dollars.

CALLAHAN. Wha . . . a . . . t?

BRODY. This stuff was worth thirty to forty thousand dollars.

LEWIS. It was? Charlie said it was mostly fake.

BRODY. (*Takes list from* DAKIS.) Look! Here's the list! See for yourself! (LEWIS *looks at it, his face drops.*)

MCLEOD. Lewis, you've been robbed. (LEWIS *nods.*)

BRODY. Where does Charlie live?

LEWIS. 129th Street, West. I know the house. I don't know the number. . . . I can show it to you. (LIEUTENANT *enters* U. L. *door, crosses* D. C.)

BRODY. Fine. (DAKIS *crosses to washroom, opens door, nods to* BARNES, *who brings* CHARLIE *back into room to bench* D. R.)

CALLAHAN. That's using your . . . (*Taps his head.*) tokas, Lewis.

O'BRIEN. Hello, Chief!

BRODY. (*Moving* U. S.) Hi, Lieutenant!

LIEUTENANT. (*Crossing to* LEWIS, *looking around.*) Busy house!

O'BRIEN. Yes, sir, we're bouncin', all of a sudden.

CALLAHAN. John! Got your car here? (O'BRIEN *nods.*) Run us over? We're gonna hit this bum's flat, Chief.

LIEUTENANT. (*Squints at* LEWIS.) What's your name?

LEWIS. Lewis Abbott.

CALLAHAN. (*Shows* LIEUTENANT *the jimmy.*) Look at this . . . (*Shows him gun.*) and this.

LIEUTENANT. Loaded?

CALLAHAN. Yeah.

BRODY. (*Indicating* CHARLIE.) The other burglar.

LIEUTENANT. (*Crossing to* CHARLIE *on bench.*) What's your name?

CHARLIE. (*As* BARNES *prods him to his feet.*) Gennini. I don't know nothing about this, Lieutenant. I was . . .

LIEUTENANT. Print him!

CALLAHAN. Yes, sir.

LIEUTENANT. Who made the collar?

BRODY. Uniform arrest. Patrolman Barnes.

LIEUTENANT. (*To* BARNES.) Nice goin'!

MCLEOD. (*Indicating* KURT *to* LIEUTENANT.) Kurt Schneider. Turned himself in.

LIEUTENANT. Mm! That mouthpiece of his got hold of me downstairs, chewed my ear off. I wanna have a talk with you. (*Beckons him into his office* R. *Crosses to office.*)

DAKIS. Charlie, on your feet! Let's go. (*Leads* CHARLIE *over to fingerprint board and "prints" him.*)

MCLEOD. (*In* LIEUTENANT'S *office, indicates* ARTHUR.) Kindred. The Pritchett complaint.

LIEUTENANT. Admission?

MCLEOD. Yes.

LIEUTENANT. Step inside, lad.—In there. (*Indicates anteroom off* R. ARTHUR *exists off* R. *To* MCLEOD.) Shut the door. (MCLEOD *shuts door to squad room.* LIEUTENANT *takes off his hat and jacket, tosses them onto coatrack.*) Oh, Schneider—what's your personal angle?

MCLEOD. (*Subtly mimics* LIEUTENANT'S *speech.*) Personal angle! None. Why?

LIEUTENANT. (*Looks up sharply.*) His mouthpiece hinted at something or other.

MCLEOD. Fishing expedition.

LIEUTENANT. You sure?

MCLEOD. Sure, I'm sure. What did Mr. Sims imply?

LIEUTENANT. (*Takes off his shoulder holster, hangs it on rack, transferring revolver to his hip pocket.*) Just vague hints.

MCLEOD. You can write those on the air!

LIEUTENANT. What have you got? (*Takes off his shirt, hangs it up.*)

MCLEOD. Girl—Miss Harris in the hospital. Critical. I called the D. A.'s office. I'm taking Schneider over to the hospital for a positive identification. I got a corroborating witness. I phoned her. She's on her way over here. And I want to get a signed statement from Schneider.

LIEUTENANT. How?

MCLEOD. Persuasion.

LIEUTENANT. Keep your big mitts off. That's an order.

MCLEOD. Were you ever in those railroad flats of his? Did you ever see that kitchen table—covered by a filthy blood-stained oil-cloth on which Kurt Schneider performs his delicate operations?

LIEUTENANT. (*Crosses to desk No. 3, opens drawer, takes out shaving articles and towel. Crosses back to* R. *of* MCLEOD.) This is an impersonal business! Your moral indignation is beginning to give me a quick pain in the butt. You got a Messianic complex. You want to be the judge and the jury, too. Well, you can't do it. It says so in the book. I don't like lawyers coming in here with photos. It marks my squad lousy. I don't like it—and I won't have it. You understand?

MCLEOD. Yes, sir.

LIEUTENANT. Can't you say, "Yes, sir," without making it sound like an insult?

MCLEOD. Yes, sir.

LIEUTENANT. You're too damn superior. That's your trouble. For the record, I don't like you any more'n you like me; but you got a value here and I need you on my squad. That's the only reason you're not wearing a white badge again.

MCLEOD. (*Reaches in his pocket for his shield.*) You wouldn't want it back now, would you?

LIEUTENANT. When I do, I'll ask for it.

MCLEOD. Because you can have it—with instructions.

LIEUTENANT. Get what you can out of Schneider, but no rough-house! You know the policy of this administration.

MCLEOD. I don't hold with it.

LIEUTENANT. What the hell ice does that cut?

MCLEOD. I don't believe in coddling criminals.

LIEUTENANT. Who tells you to?

MCLEOD. You do. The whole damn system does.

LIEUTENANT. Sometimes, McLeod, you talk like a maniac.

MCLEOD. (*Starts to speak.*) May I . . . ?

LIEUTENANT. No. You got your orders. That's all.

MCLEOD. May I have the keys to the files, *sir?*

LIEUTENANT. You got to have the last word, don't you? (*Throws keys on desk No. 3, exit off* R. JOE *enters* U. L. *door, crosses to table* U. C.)

DAKIS. (*Finishes fingerprinting* CHARLIE, *waves him to washroom.*)

Charlie, wash up! In there! (CHARLIE *crosses to washroom, starts to close door.* BARNES *stops it.*)

JOE. (*To* BRODY.) How many burglaries?

BRODY. Nine or ten. (*Starting* L. *A handsome young girl* [SUSAN] *enters* U. L., *stands at gate, looking about for help.*)

JOE. Any important names? Any good addresses?

BRODY. (*Moans.*) We don't know yet. You'll get it. Don't rush us, will you, Joey? (*Exit* D. L. *door.*)

CALLAHAN. (*Crosses up to gate.*) Yes, Miss?

SUSAN. May I see Detective McLeod?

CALLAHAN. He's busy. Anything I can do for you? (*He scrutinizes her.*) I seen your face before?

SUSAN. No.

CALLAHAN. I never forget a face. (JOE *looks at her, then wanders into* LIEUTENANT'S *office.*)

SUSAN. You probably saw my sister.

CALLAHAN. Who's your sister?

SUSAN. Please tell him Miss Susan Carmichael is here.

CALLAHAN. Yes, Miss. Just a minute. (*Puts cards away in his files* U. R.)

MCLEOD. (*In* LIEUTENANT'S *office, examining burglary sheets, still fuming at* LIEUTENANT.) Ignorant, gross ward-heeler! Why don't you print the truth for once, Yussel?

JOE. Which truth?—Yours, his, theirs, mine?

MCLEOD. *The* truth.

JOE. Oh, that one? Who would know it? If it came up and blew in your ear, who would know it?

CALLAHAN. (*Pokes head into doorway of* LIEUTENANT'S *office.*) Kid outside for you! (*Sits chair below desk No.* 2.)

JOE. A nice tall kid. (*Watching* MCLEOD, *who is going through files.*) I love these kids today. I got a nephew, seventeen, six-foot-three, blond hair, blue eyes. Science tells us the turn of the century all the kids are going to be seven foot tall. Seven foot . . . that's for me.

MCLEOD. No time for a philosophic discussion today, Yussel (*Starts for outer office through door to squad room.*)

JOE. (*Following.*) Don't throw water on McLeod. He goes rabid.

BARNES. (*To* CHARLIE, *as he comes out of washroom.*) O. K., Charlie. Come with me. (*They exit through gate* U. L. CALLAHAN *takes* LEWIS *out* U. L., *followed by* CHARLIE *and* BARNES.)

MCLEOD. (*To* O'BRIEN, *who is following* CHARLIE *out*.) Hey, John, I need eight or ten fellas up here for a line-up. Ask a couple of the men downstairs to get into civvies!

O'BRIEN. Line-up? Sure. (*Exits* U. L. JOE *sits* U. S. *table in front of windows*.)

MCLEOD. (*Coming down to* L. *desk No.* 2, *addresses* SUSAN *at gate*.) Miss Carmichael?

SUSAN. Yes. I'm Susan Carmichael.

MCLEOD. Come in, please!

SUSAN. (*Enters through gate, crosses down to* L. *of desk No.* 2, *facing* MCLEOD.) Are you the officer who phoned?

MCLEOD. (R. *of desk No.* 2.) Yes. I'm Detective McLeod.

SUSAN. (*Frantic*.) Where's Arthur? What happened to him? What's this about?

MCLEOD. Did you contact your sister?

SUSAN. (*Hesitating*.) N . . . no!

MCLEOD. Why not?

SUSAN. I couldn't reach her.

MCLEOD. Where is she?

SUSAN. Visiting some friends in Connecticut. I don't know the address. Where's Arthur? Is he all right?

MCLEOD. Yes. He's inside. How well do you know Arthur Kindred?

SUSAN. Very. All my life. We lived next door to each other in Ann Arbor.

MCLEOD. Kind of a wild boy, wasn't he? (BRODY *enters door* D. L., *crosses to below rail—listens*.)

SUSAN. Arthur? Not at all. He was always very serious. Why?

MCLEOD. Did he give your sister any money?

SUSAN. My sister earns $25 an hour. She's a very successful model. She averages $300 to $400 a week for herself. Will you please tell me what this is about?

MCLEOD. Let me ask the questions. Do you mind?

SUSAN. Sorry!

MCLEOD. Arthur was in the Navy?

SUSAN. Five years.

MCLEOD. He got a dishonorable discharge.

SUSAN. What are you talking about? (BRODY *becomes interested, edges over, listening*.)

MCLEOD. That's a question.

SUSAN. You didn't punctuate it.
MCLEOD. Correction. (*Smiles.*) Did he?
SUSAN. Arthur was cited four times. He got the silver star. He carried a sailor up three decks of a burning ship. He had two ships sunk under him. He floated around once in the Pacific Ocean for seventeen hours with sharks all around him. When they picked him up, he was out of his head, trying to climb onto a concrete platform that wasn't there. He was in the hospital for ten weeks after that. Any more questions?
MCLEOD. What is his relationship to your sister?
SUSAN. I told you, we all grew up together.
MCLEOD. Is he in love with her?
SUSAN. My sister is one of the most beautiful girls in New York. A lot of men are in love with her. May I talk to Arthur now, please?
MCLEOD. He didn't give her any money, then?
SUSAN. No.
MCLEOD. Did he give it to you?
SUSAN. Are you kidding?
MCLEOD. I'm afraid not. Your sister's boy-friend is in trouble.
SUSAN. What trouble?
MCLEOD. He's a thief.
SUSAN. Who says so?
MCLEOD. He does.
SUSAN. I don't believe you.
MCLEOD. Sit down. (*Calls through door of* LIEUTENANT'S *office to room off* R. SUSAN *sits chair below desk No.* 2.) Arthur! (ARTHUR *comes through* LIEUTENANT'S *office into squad room, sees* SUSAN.)
SUSAN. (*Rises.*) Jiggs! What happened?
ARTHUR. (*Crosses* D. *to her.*) Suzy! (*Glares indignantly at* MCLEOD.) Did you have to drag children into this?
MCLEOD. Now, Jiggs!
ARTHUR. Susan, you shouldn't have come here.
SUSAN. What happened?
ARTHUR. I took some money.
SUSAN. Who from?
ARTHUR. The man I worked for.
SUSAN. But why, Jiggs, why?
ARTHUR. None of your business.

BRODY. Say, Jim!

MCLEOD. Yes? *(Steps up to desk No. 2 for a moment, talks to* BRODY *sotto voce.* ARTHUR *whispers hoarsely, urgently.)*

ARTHUR. *(To* SUSAN, *who is* D. R.*)* Suzy, go home—quick—go home—get out of here. And don't say anything to anyone.

SUSAN. *(Whispers.)* Jiggs, what happened? Have you got a lawyer?

ARTHUR. No!

SUSAN. I'll phone Joy and tell her.

ARTHUR. Do you want to get her involved? You want to ruin her career?

SUSAN. *(Whispering.)* But, Jiggs ——

ARTHUR. *(Whispering.)* Get out of here, will you? (MCLEOD *returns.)*

MCLEOD. Well, young lady—satisfied?

SUSAN. How much did he take?

MCLEOD. $480.

ARTHUR. What's the difference? Will you please tell her to go home, Officer? She's only a kid.

SUSAN. I'm not. I wish you'd . . .

ARTHUR. She shouldn't be here. She's got nothing to do with this.

MCLEOD. All right, young lady. I'm sorry to have bothered you. Have your sister get in touch with me as soon as you hear from her.

ARTHUR. What for? Don't you do it, Suzy—you don't have to. *(To* MCLEOD.*)* You're not going to get her involved in this.

MCLEOD. You shut up! *(To* SUSAN.*)* O. K. *(Motions* SUSAN *to go. She bites her lip to keep from crying, and goes out* U. L. *door.)*

BRODY. *(To* ARTHUR.*)* Is it true that you carried a wounded sailor on your shoulders up three decks of a burning ship? (MCLEOD *gets coffee from* U. C. *table.)*

ARTHUR. Yes.

BRODY. Pretty good.

ARTHUR. Could I have that drink now? Please!

BRODY. Yeah. (ARTHUR *sits bench* R. BRODY *crosses over to his files* U. R., *takes out bottle of whisky, pours a drink.* MCLEOD *crosses over to* KURT D. L., *sipping coffee from container.)*

MCLEOD. You're looking well, Kurt. (DAKIS *sits table* U. C.*)*

KURT. Could be better.

MCLEOD. (*Sits at typewriter desk No. 1, inserts sheet of paper.*) How's the farm?
KURT. All right!
MCLEOD. Wasn't there a drought in Jersey this year? (*Starts to type statement.*)
KURT. I irrigate my crops. I've got plenty of water.
MCLEOD. What do you raise?
KURT. Cabbage . . . lettuce . . . kale! Truck stuff!
MCLEOD. (*Typing.*) That's the life. Picturesque country, North Jersey. Nice hills, unexpected!
KURT. Yes. How're things with you?
MCLEOD. This is one business never has a depression.
BRODY. (*Comes down, hands drink to* ARTHUR *on bench,* D. R.) Here you are, son!
MCLEOD. (*Drinks—surveys his container.*) They make pretty good cup of coffee across the street.
KURT. So-so.
MCLEOD. (*Types.*) When I retire I'm going to buy myself a little farm like yours, settle down. Does it really pay for itself?
KURT. If you work it.
MCLEOD. How much can a man average a year?
KURT. Varies. Two thousand a good year.
MCLEOD. Clear? That's pretty good.
KURT. Sometimes you lose a crop.
MCLEOD. How long you had that farm, Kurt? (*Stops typing.*)
KURT. Eleven years.
MCLEOD. And you average two thousand a year?
KURT. . . . ???
MCLEOD. Then how'd you manage to accumulate $56,000 in the bank, Kurt? H'm? (*Silence.*) H'm, Kurt? How?
KURT. Who says I have?
MCLEOD. I do. I checked. $56,000. That's a lot of kale. (*Takes notebook from his pocket.*) You got it in four banks. Passaic—Oakdale—two in Newark. Here are the figures. How'd you get that money, Kurt?
KURT. I got it honestly.
MCLEOD. How? How?
KURT. I don't have to tell you that.
MCLEOD. Oh, come on, Kurt. How? (KURT *shakes head.*) Make

it easy for yourself. You still running that abortion mill, aren't you?

KURT. My name is Kurt Schneider—I live in Oakdale, New Jersey. That's all I have to answer.

MCLEOD. (*Rise.*) You operated on Miss Harris, didn't you?

KURT. No, I did not!

MCLEOD. She identified your picture. (KURT *shrugs shoulders.* MCLEOD *hands him paper he has typed.*) Sign that, Kurt!

KURT. What is it?

MCLEOD. An admission.

KURT. You think I'm crazy?

MCLEOD. We've got you dead to rights. Make it easy for yourself.

KURT. I'm not saying anything more, on advice of counsel!

MCLEOD. I'm getting impatient! You better talk, Kurt.

KURT. I'm standing on my Constitutional rights!

MCLEOD. (*Rising, moving above desk No. 1 and down to* KURT.) Hold your hats, boys, here we go again. (*Looking down on* KURT *from behind him.*) You know you're lucky, Kurt. You've gotten away with it once before. But the postman rings twice. And this time we've got you, Kurt. Why don't you cop a plea? While you can. . . . Miss Harris is waiting for you. We're going to visit her in the hospital. She's anxious to see you. And what you don't know is . . . there was a corroborating witness, and she's downstairs ready to identify you right now. . . . You're getting pale, Kurt. (KURT *laughs softly to himself.*) What are you laughing at?

KURT. Nothing.

MCLEOD. That's right! That's just what you've got to laugh about —nothing. You're on the bottom of this joke.

KURT. Maybe I am. Maybe I'm not. Maybe somebody else is.

MCLEOD. What's that mean?

KURT. I know why you're out to get me.

MCLEOD. Why? . . . (KURT *shakes head.*)

KURT. You know why.

MCLEOD. Why? Why, Kurt? This is your last chance. Do you want to talk?

KURT. My name is Kurt Schneider—I live in Oakdale, New Jersey. That's all I'm obliged to say by law.

MCLEOD. You should have been a lawyer, Kurt. A Philadelphia

lawyer. (*Crosses to rail, shouts downstairs.*) Gus, O. K. on the line-up.

GUS. (*Off, shouts up.*) O. K., Jim, be right with you. (*Starts to sing off.*)

MCLEOD. (*To* DAKIS.) Nick, put on your hat and coat for a line-up. (DAKIS *exits off* D. L. *for coat.* BRODY *crosses down to* ARTHUR, *again seated bench* R. ARTHUR *hands him the glass.*)

ARTHUR. Thanks. (*Pause.* BRODY *looks at* ARTHUR *with sweet compassion.*)

BRODY. My boy was in the Navy, too. *The Juneau.* Know her?

ARTHUR. She was a cruiser.

BRODY. Yeah.

ARTHUR. Didn't she go down with all hands? In the Pacific?

BRODY. There were only ten survivors. He wasn't one of them.

ARTHUR. Too bad.

BRODY. Yeah! He was my only boy. It's something you never get over. You never believe it. You keep waiting for a bell to ring. Phone, door. Sometimes I hear a voice on the street, or see a young fellow from the back, the set of his shoulders—like you—for a minute it's him. Your whole life becomes like a dream . . . a walking dream.

ARTHUR. Maybe he was one of the lucky ones.

BRODY. Don't say that. (*Entrance of line-up from hall* U. L. KEOGH, KURT, O'BRIEN, *and* CALLAHAN *enter and stand down* L. *to upper* R. GALLAGHER *from* LIEUTENANT'S *office* R., *and stands* C., BRODY *following him, standing to his* R. DAKIS *enters door down* L. *and stands front of desk No. 1.* GALLAGHER *and* BRODY *enter a little later, as indicated in stage directions.*)

ARTHUR. Why not?

BRODY. Because it wouldn't make sense then.

ARTHUR. Does it?

BRODY. Yes. (*Fiercely.*) Goddamn it! Yes. (GALLAGHER *enters from* LIEUTENANT'S *office anteroom* R. *Crosses into squad room.*)

MCLEOD. Say, Lou! Will you put on your hat and coat for a line-up? (*The men in the line-up are in civilian clothes, they are laughing and kidding.* BRODY *gets hat and coat from* LIEUTENANT'S *office hat tree.*) O. K., Kurt. Put on your hat. Pick your spot. End? Middle? Any place. No alibis later. (*Line-up from* U. R. *to* D. L. *desk No. 1.* WILLY *stands to* R. *end of line-up.*)

CALLAHAN. Say, Gus, you look almost human in civvies.

GUS. Wish I could say the same for you.
CALLAHAN. You could if you were as big a liar as I am. (DAKIS *and others laugh.*)
MCLEOD. (*Calling to off-stage hall* U. L.) All right! Come in, please. (MISS HATCH *enters* U. L., *wearing a new fur stole.*) How do you do, Miss Hatch?
MISS HATCH. I'm fine, thank you. (*Crosses down to* MCLEOD R. MCLEOD *scrutinizes her, frowns.*) What'sa . . . ?
MCLEOD. (*Indicating furpiece.*) Rushing the season, aren't you?
MISS HATCH. (*Laughs nervously.*) Oh!
MCLEOD. New?
MISS HATCH. Yes.
MCLEOD. Mink?
MISS HATCH. Uh-uh! Dyed squirrel! Looks real, though, doesn't it?
MCLEOD. It was nice of you to come down and help us. We appreciate that.
MISS HATCH. Don't mention it. Let's just get it over with, huh? I got an engagement. What do I —— (*She looks about for ashtray for her cigarette.*)
MCLEOD. Throw it on the floor. (*She does so. He steps on it.*) You have your instructions?
MISS HATCH. Yeah. I look at them all, then touch the one on the shoulder. (*He nods. She walks slowly down line from* R. *to* L., *nervously scrutinizing the faces a little too quickly to be convincing. Turns to* MCLEOD.) He isn't here.
MCLEOD. (*Crossing to* C.) You haven't looked.
MISS HATCH. I looked. Of course I did.
CALLAHAN. It's the new look.
MCLEOD. Just look, will you? Not at me. Over there.
MISS HATCH. I don't recognize anyone. I never saw any of these guys in my life before.
MCLEOD. (*Steps toward her.*) You identified a picture of one of these men. . . .
MISS HATCH. (*Steps toward him.*) What are you trying to do . . . make me give you a wrong identification? Well, I ain't gonna do it.
MCLEOD. (*Rubs his thumb and forefinger.*) Do you know what this means?
MISS HATCH. Yeah. That's your cut on the side.

MCLEOD. You're fresh. (*Phone rings desk No. 2.* BRODY *answers it.*)
BRODY. 21st Squad. Brody. (*Conversation sotto voce.*)
MCLEOD. I've a good mind to prefer charges against you.
MISS HATCH. (*Screams at him.*) That's what I get for coming all the way downtown to help you! The cops are all the same. Give you a badge and you think you can push the world around.
MCLEOD. You identified one of these men . . . now, goddam it, point him out or I'm going to throw you into the clink!
MISS HATCH. You'll do what? (BRODY *hangs up phone, calls* MCLEOD *to one side.*)
BRODY. (D. R.) Jim!
MCLEOD. (*Crossing to* BRODY.) Yes?
BRODY. (*In subdued tones.*) That was the D. A.'s office. The Harris girl died.
MCLEOD. When?
BRODY. A couple of hours ago.
MCLEOD. Why weren't we informed?
BRODY. I don't know.
MCLEOD. There goes the case.
BRODY. The D. A. says just go through the motions. He can't get an indictment now. Just book him and forget it, he says.
MCLEOD. Yes. Forget it. Let him go. Let him fill the morgues. (*Crosses to* KURT.) Congratulations, Kurt. The girl died. Sit down. All right, Miss Hatch. You've earned your fur-piece. I hope you'll enjoy it.
MISS HATCH. (*Crosses to* MCLEOD D. L.) You can't talk to me that way. I'm no tramp that you can talk to me that way. Who the hell do you think you are anyway?
MCLEOD. Get out! Take a couple of drop-dead pills. Get lost.
MISS HATCH. You big cheese! I'm going to see my lawyer about you. (*She goes* U. L.)
MCLEOD. All right, men, thank you. (*They go, as they came in, except* DAKIS. *We hear following conversation from the men.*)
GUS. I was waiting for her to put the finger on you, boy.
DAKIS. (*Crosses* U. R., *exit into washroom.*) Me? Do I look like an ice-tong man?
O'BRIEN. Regular Sarah Heartburn.
CALLAHAN. One minute more we'd have gotten the witches' scene

from *Macbeth*. Come on. We've got to hit this bum's flat. (WILLY, *the janitor, has entered* U. L. *with men for the line-up.*)

WILLY. (*Sweeping vigorously, muttering all the while.*) Now look at this joint, will you? You filthy slobs. You live in a stable. (*To* SHOPLIFTER.) Come on, get up. (*She rises. He sweeps right through her.*) Wouldn't think I swept it out an hour ago. Boy, I'd like to see the homes you bums live in. Pig-pens, I bet. (*Exit* U. L.)

MCLEOD. (*Crosses up to duty chart, takes it off wall, crosses down to desk No. 2 with it, murmuring for* JOE'S *benefit, sits.*) Why am I wasting my life here? I could make more driving a hack. I like books. I like music. I've got a wonderful, wonderful wife—I could get a dozen jobs would give me more time to enjoy the good things of life. I should have my head examined. All this work. These hours! What for? It's a phoney. (*He removes letters spelling out* GALLAGHER *and* DAKIS, *places them in drawer, takes out other letters, inserts his name and* BRODY'S.)

JOE. (*Comes down.*) Was she reached, you think?

MCLEOD. What do *you* think?

JOE. I don't know.

MCLEOD. (*Groans.*) Oh, Yussel.

JOE. I don't know.

MCLEOD. This is a phoney. The thieves and murderers could have written the penal code themselves. Your democracy, Yussel, is a Rube Goldberg contraption. An elaborate machine a block long—you set it all in motion, 3000 wheels turn, it goes ping. (*He crosses up again, replaces chart on wall.*)

JOE. That's what's great about it. That's what I love. It's so confused, it's wonderful. (*Crosses up to* MCLEOD.) After all, Seamus, guilt and innocence!—The epistemological question! Just the knowing . . . the mere knowing . . . the ability to ken. Maybe he didn't do it. Maybe she can't identify him. How do you know? (BRODY *enters squad room from files in* LIEUTENANT'S *office, sits at desk No. 2.*)

MCLEOD. How do you know anything? You got a nose you can smell, you've got taste buds you can taste, you've got nerve endings you can feel, and, theoretically, you've got intelligence . . . you can judge.

JOE. Ah-ha! That's where it breaks down!

MCLEOD. (*To* BRODY.) Got an aspirin? (BRODY *hands him box of aspirin,* MCLEOD *crosses over into* LIEUTENANT'S *office,* JOE *follows him.*)

JOE. That's where it breaks down. I was talking to Judge Mendez today. He just got on the bench last year, you know. Twenty-nine years a successful lawyer. He thought this would be a cinch. He's lost forty pounds. He's nervous as a cat. His wife thinks he has a mistress. He has. The law. (*He sits* D. L. *of office.*) Said to me today: "Joe, I've got to sentence a man to death tomorrow. How can I do it? Who am I to judge? It takes a God to know! To really know!"

MCLEOD. (*In Lieutenant's office, gets glass of water from cooler* R., *tosses aspirin into his mouth.*) Bunk!

JOE. I'm quoting Judge Mendez.

MCLEOD. Then he's a corrupt man himself. All lawyers are, anyway. I say hang all the lawyers, and let justice triumph. (*Washes down aspirin with a drink, sits swivel chair, takes off tie, rolls up sleeve, slowly reflecting.*) Evil has a stench of its own. A child can spot it. I know . . . I know, Yussel. My own father was one of them. No good he was . . . possessed. Every day and every night of my childhood I saw and heard him abuse and torment my mother. I saw that sadistic son-of-a-bitch of a father of mine with that criminal mind of his drive my mother straight into a lunatic asylum. She died in a lunatic asylum. (*Pause.*) Yes, I know it when I smell it. I learned it early and deep. I was fourteen and alone in the world. I made war on it. Every time I look at one of these babies, I see my father's face! (*Phone rings in outer office, desk No.* 2. BRODY *answers.*)

BRODY. 21st Squad. Brody. (*Pause.*) Lock the door. Don't let him out! I'll be right over. (*Rushing to* LIEUTENANT'S *office for his hat and coat.*) Say, Jim, there's a guy at O'Donovan's bar with a badge and gun, arresting a woman. Claims he's a cop. Might be, might be a shake-down. I'll be right back. Catch the phone for me! (*Takes his gun out of drawer desk No.* 2 *and runs off.* DAKIS *comes out of washroom, sits* L. *of table* U. C. *Reads newspaper.*)

JOE. (*Runs after him.*) Might be shooting. Wait for me, baby! (*Exits* U. L. MCLEOD *comes out of* LIEUTENANT'S *office.*)

MCLEOD. (*To* KURT. *Crosses* C. *above desk No.* 2.) You're a lucky man, Kurt. Kissed in your cradle by a vulture. So the girl died, Kurt.

KURT. That's too bad.

MCLEOD. (*Crossing to* KURT, *seated* D. L.) What have you got, Kurt, in place of a conscience? (KURT *starts to speak.*) Don't answer!—I know—a lawyer. I ought to fall on you like the sword of God.

KURT. The sword's got two edges. You could cut your own throat.

MCLEOD. (*Crossing to* D. C. *Takes out cigarette, turns away to light it.*) Look! The gate's open! While I'm lighting my cigarette —why don't you run for it? One second, you'll be out in the street.

KURT. I'll go free, anyway. Why should I run?

MCLEOD. Give me the little pleasure—of putting a hole in the back of your head.

KURT. You wouldn't do that. Talk!

MCLEOD. Is it?

KURT. You're an intelligent man. You're not foolish.

MCLEOD. Try me, Kurt. Why don't you? Go ahead, dance down that hall!

KURT. (*Smiles, shakes his head.*) Soon as you book me, I'm out on bail. When I go to trial, they couldn't convict me in a million years. You know that. Even if I were guilty, which I'm not. . . . The girl is dead. There are no witnesses. That's the law.

MCLEOD. You've been well briefed. You know your catechism.

KURT. Sure, I know more than my catechism!

MCLEOD. What, for example? (*Crosses back to* KURT.) What, Kurt? What goes on under that monkey-skull of yours, I wonder! (KURT *is silent.*) On your feet! (KURT *looks up at* MCLEOD'S *face, is frightened by its almost mad intensity.* MCLEOD *roars at him.*) Get up!! (KURT *rises.*) Go in there! (*Points to* LIEUTENANT'S *office.* KURT *goes into* LIEUTENANT'S *office.* MCLEOD *follows him, shuts door.*) Sit down, Kurt. (KURT *sits* L. *of desk No. 3, back to audience.*) I'm going to give you a piece of advice. When the courts and the juries and the judges let you free this time, get out of New York. Go to Georgia. They won't extradite criminals to us. So, you see, Kurt—take my advice, go to Georgia, or go to hell, you murdering son-of-a-bitch, but you butcher one more girl in this city—and law or no law, I'll find you and I'll put a bullet in the back of your head, and I'll drop your body in the East River, and I'll go home and I'll sleep sweetly.

KURT. You have to answer to the law the same as I. You don't frighten me. Now, I'll give you some advice. I've got plenty on you, too. . . . I know why you're so vindictive. And you watch your step! Because I happen to have friends, too, downtown . . . with pull . . . lots of pull. . . .

MCLEOD. Have you? What do you know? Aren't you the big shot! Pull! Have you got any friends with *push!* Like *that!* . . . for example! (*Kicks him*—KURT *goes over, chair and all.*)

KURT. Cut that out! You let me alone now. . . . (MCLEOD *grabs him by the lapels, pulls him to his feet.*) You let me go! Let me go!

MCLEOD. No, Kurt! Everybody else is going to let you go. You got it all figured . . . exactly. The courts—the juries—the judges—(*Slaps him.*) everybody except me. . . . (KURT *starts to resist,* MCLEOD *hits him in the belly.* KURT *crumples to the floor.*) Why didn't you obey your lawyer and keep your mouth shut? All right! Get up, Kurt! Come on! Get up!

KURT. (*Moaning and writhing.*) I can't . . . I can't. . . . Something inside . . . broke! (*He calls feebly.*) Help! (*Very loud.*) HELP!

MCLEOD. Get up! You're all right. Get up! (LIEUTENANT MONOGHAN *enters door* U. R. GALLAGHER *enters door* U. R.)

LIEUTENANT. What's going on? (*He sees* KURT, *goes to him, bends down.*)

KURT. Inside! It broke. He hurt me. . . . (DAKIS *rushes in from squad room.*)

LIEUTENANT. Take it easy, son, you'll be all right.

KURT. I feel terrible.

LIEUTENANT. Nick! Quick! Get an ambulance.

DAKIS. Yes, sir. (*Goes to phone, desk No.* 3, *puts in a call.*)

LIEUTENANT. Did he resist you?

MCLEOD. No.

LIEUTENANT. No? You lunatic! Didn't I just get through warning you to lay off? (*To* KURT, *who is on floor, moaning in agony.*)

KURT. (*Gasping for breath.*) He tried to kill me!

LIEUTENANT. Why should he do that?

KURT. Tami Giacoppetti! . . . Same thing! . . . She got him after me, too. . . . Tami Giacoppetti. . . .

LIEUTENANT. (*Leans over* KURT.) What? Tami Giacoppetti? Who's he? What about him? (*Puts ear to* KURT'S *mouth.*) A little louder! Just try and talk a little louder, lad. (KURT'S *eyes close, his head falls back. He is unconscious. To* GALLAGHER.) Wet some towels! (GALLAGHER *rushes to washroom.* DAKIS *loosens* KURT'S *collar, tries to bring him to.* LIEUTENANT *rises, confronts* MCLEOD, *glaring at him.*) Who's Tami Giacoppetti?

MCLEOD. I've no idea.

LIEUTENANT. What's the pitch here, McLeod?

MCLEOD. He needled me. He got fresh. He begged for it, and I let him have it. That's all. (GALLAGHER *returns with wet towels.* DAKIS *takes them from him, applies them to* KURT'S *head.*)

LIEUTENANT. Don't con me! That ain't all. Come on! Let's have it! What about this Tami Giacoppetti?

MCLEOD. I never heard of him.

GALLAGHER. Giacoppetti? I know him. A black market guy. Runs a creep joint in the village.

LIEUTENANT. This could be a very hot potato. If this man's hurt, the big brass'll be down here throwin' questions at me. And I'm going to have the answers. What plays between you two guys? What's he got on you? What's the clout?

MCLEOD. Nothing.

LIEUTENANT. Then what was his mouthpiece yellin' and screamin' about?

MCLEOD. Red herring. Red, red herring!

LIEUTENANT. (*Stands.*) Then I'm gonna goddamn well find out for myself. There's something kinky about this. McLeod, if you're concealing something from me, I'll have your head on a plate. (*To* GALLAGHER.) This Giacoppetti! Find him and bring him in!

GALLAGHER. Yes, sir. (*Goes out through squad room.*)

LIEUTENANT. (*Calls after him.*) My car's downstairs. Use it.

GALLAGHER. Yes, sir. (*Exit* U. L. LIEUTENANT *bends down to* KURT. MCLEOD, *grim-faced, lights another cigarette.*)

CURTAIN

ACT II

SCENE: *The scene is the same, 7:30 is the time by the clock on the wall.*

AT RISE: *The lawyer,* ENDICOTT SIMS, *is closeted in* LIEUTENANT'S *office, scolding* LIEUTENANT *and* MCLEOD. SIMS *sits above desk No. 3,* LIEUTENANT *just below it,* MCLEOD *below and to* L. *of it. Outside,* SHOPLIFTER *is reading the comics.* ARTHUR *is seated on bench* D. R., *quietly, his head bowed in thought.* DAKIS, *the janitor, and* GUS *are in a huddle, whispering, glancing over toward* LIEUTENANT'S *door.* BRODY *is* D. L., *talking sotto voce to an excited man and woman,* MR. AND MRS. FEENEY, *who are glaring at a tough-looking specimen, seated* D. L. *by desk No. 1.*

SIMS. How dare you take the law in your own hands? Who are you to constitute yourself a court of last appeal? (*Phone bell.*)
LIEUTENANT. (*Trying to appease.*) Now, Counsellor . . . (BRODY *goes from desk No. 1 to desk No. 2 to answer phone.*)
BRODY. 21st Squad, Detective Brody. . . . Yeah. . . . Yeah.
SIMS. No. Lieutenant! This is a felony. I'm going to press a felony assault here. So help me, I'm going to see you in jail!
MCLEOD. On which side of the bars, Counsellor?
SIMS. Be careful. I'm an attorney and an officer of the court, and I don't like that talk.
MCLEOD. I'm an officer of the peace and I don't like collusion.
SIMS. (*A step to* MCLEOD.) What do you mean by that?
MCLEOD. By that I mean collusion. Subornation of witnesses, Counsellor.
SIMS. What the devil are you talking about?
MCLEOD. Subornation. I'm charging you with subornation.
SIMS. Your lips are blistering with lies.
MCLEOD. Praise from an expert! I had a witness here today against your client whom you bought off, Counsellor.
SIMS. That's so absurd I'm not even going to answer it.
MCLEOD. I'll prove it.

LIEUTENANT. All right! Cut it! Cut it out. Enough's enough.

SIMS. I intend to carry this to the Commissioner.

LIEUTENANT. (*Pushes phone, desk No. 3, over.*) Call him now. That's your privilege.

SIMS. And don't think you're entirely free of blame in this, Lieutenant.

LIEUTENANT. Me? What have I ——?

SIMS. I warned you that personal motives are involved in this case, and I was afraid this was going to happen. You should have taken the necessary steps to prevent it. Luckily, I came armed with photos and affidavits.

LIEUTENANT. Mystery! Mystery! What motives?

MCLEOD. Yes. Why don't you tell us? I'd like to hear. Let's get it out in the open. What are these motives?

SIMS. It is not to my client's interests to reveal them at this moment.

MCLEOD. (*To* LIEUTENANT.) Legal bull!

LIEUTENANT. I'm beginning to think so.

SIMS. Sure. One hand washes the other. (BRODY *knocks at door of* LIEUTENANT'S *office.*)

LIEUTENANT. Come in!

BRODY. Phone, Lieutenant.

LIEUTENANT. (*Picks up phone on desk No. 3.*) 21st Squad, Lieutenant Monoghan. . . . Yeah. . . . Yeah. . . .

SIMS. On what evidence do you make these serious charges?

MCLEOD. The evidence of my intelligent observation.

SIMS. Insufficient, incompetent and irrelevant.

LIEUTENANT. Sh! Sh!

SIMS. You're pretty cagey, McLeod, but your tactics don't fool me for a second. You are not going to duck out of this so easily. You are in a position of responsibility here and you have got to answer for your actions. You can't use your badge for personal vengeance. That doesn't go. The public isn't your servant. You're theirs. You're going to be broken for this.

MCLEOD. Go ahead! Break me! You're worse than the criminals you represent, Counsellor. (*Rises, faces* SIMS.) You're so damn respectable. Yet look at you! The clothes you wear, your car downstairs, your house in Westchester, all bought with stolen money, tainted with blood.

LIEUTENANT. Shut up! I got the hospital.

SIMS. How is he?

LIEUTENANT. (*As they listen attentively.*) Yes. Yes. I see. Will you keep in touch wtih me? Let me know right away. (*Hangs up.*) See, Counsellor, it always pays to await events. There are no external lacerations on your client that would warrant a felony assault. They are now making X-ray and tests to see if there are any internal injuries. So far you haven't got a leg to stand on.

MCLEOD. No! Let him bring charges. (*To* SIMS.) Bring your felony charge. It'll give me a chance to get your client on the stand and really tear his clothes off. And yours, too, Counsellor.

LIEUTENANT. McLeod! Step outside! (MCLEOD *comes out of* LIEUTENANT'S *office.*)

BRODY. What's the score?

MCLEOD. Tempest in a teapot.

SIMS. (*Crosses down.* DAKIS *to desk No. 1.*) What kind of officer is that?

LIEUTENANT. Detectives are like fingerprints. No two alike. He has his quoiks.

SIMS. The understatement of the year.

LIEUTENANT. We all got 'em. He has a value here. He's honest. He ain't on the take. I stand up for him on that. Got no tin boxes.

SIMS. I wasn't saying he had.

LIEUTENANT. I thought you was, maybe.

SIMS. No . . .

LIEUTENANT. Then what was you saying? I guess I fumbled it.

SIMS. I can't discuss it with you.

LIEUTENANT. I'd love to discuss it with someone. Who do you suggest?

SIMS. McLeod.

LIEUTENANT. Counsellor!

SIMS. Or his wife!

LIEUTENANT. (*Looks up sharply.*) His wife? What do you mean by that?

SIMS. Never mind! Skip it!

LIEUTENANT. No. You mentioned his wife. What do you mean by that? Look! I got to get it clear up here. A little cooperation would go a long way.

SIMS. When it serves my client's interests . . . not before.

LIEUTENANT. Four years ago I threw my radio set the hell outa the window. You know why? Because, goddamn it, I hate mysteries!

SIMS. (*Smiles.*) I'm not free to discuss this, Lieutenant. (*Looks at his watch.*) Gouverneur Hospital?

LIEUTENANT. Yeah.

SIMS. I want to see my client. Will I be allowed in?

LIEUTENANT. Yeah.

SIMS. I'll be back. (*Leaves* LIEUTENANT'S *office. In squad room he pauses to confront* MCLEOD.) I'll be back. I'm not through with you.

MCLEOD. I can't wait. (SIMS *exits* U. L.)

BRODY. (*To* MCLEOD, *indicating the tough, surly-looking Crumb-bum.*) This creep was impersonating an officer.

WOMAN. I didn't know. I thought he might be a policeman. His badge looked real.

BRODY. A shake-down. After he took you outside he probably would have taken all your money and let you go. You see, that's how we get a bad reputation. Now you will appear in court at ten o'clock tomorrow morning, won't you?

WOMAN. Oh, yes.

MAN. W-e-l-l . . . tomorrow morning? But I've got a job.

WOMAN. You'll explain to your boss. You'll just take off, that's all.

MAN. But, Isabel . . .

WOMAN. He'll be there. Don't you worry. Thank you. Thank you. (*They exit* U. L.)

BRODY. I'm going down to book this Crumb-bum.

CRUMB-BUM. What did you call me?

BRODY. Crumb-bum. Come on. (*Inside,* LIEUTENANT *squints at his cigar a moment, rises, bellows:*)

LIEUTENANT. McLeod!

MCLEOD. Yes, sir? (*Crosses to* LIEUTENANT'S *door, opens it.*)

LIEUTENANT. What the hell is this about? What's he driving at? I want the truth.

MQLEOD. Lieutenant, I give you my solemn word of honor . . .

LIEUTENANT. (*Studies him, waves him away.*) Shut the door! (MCLEOD *shuts door to office, crosses to* C. *desk No.* 3, *sits. A sad-looking* GALLANTZ *appears at gate.*)

MCLEOD. Yes, sir? What can I do for you?

GALLANTZ. I want to report, someone picked my pocket.

MCLEOD. Come in!

GALLANTZ. (*Exposes his backside, revealing a patch cut out of his trousers.*) Look! They cut it right out.

MCLEOD. They work that way. With a razor blade. Sit down! Did you see the man?

GALLANTZ. No. First I knew I was in a restaurant. I ate a big meal, reached in my pocket to pay the check. Boy, I almost dropped dead. I'm lucky I'm not here under arrest myself.

MCLEOD. Yeah! (*Smiles.*) What's your name?

GALLANTZ. Gallantz, D. David.

WILLY. (*To* GALLANTZ.) Get up.

MCLEOD. Address? (WILLY *empties basket under desk No. 2 into his pail.*)

GALLANTZ. (*Rises, staring at* WILLY.) 419 West 80th Street.

WILLY. (*Muttering indignantly, paying no attention to anyone as he crosses off, door down* L.) Look at this room, will you? Wouldn't think I cleaned up an hour ago! Detectives! The brains of the department?! Couldn't find a Chinaman on Mott Street.

MCLEOD. What did you lose?

GALLANTZ. My wallet.

MCLEOD. Can you describe the wallet?

GALLANTZ. Black leather.

MCLEOD. (*On phone.*) Lost Property.

SHOPLIFTER. (*Reading paper.*) Have you got one of them two-way radio wrist-watches like Dick Tracy?

DAKIS. No.

SHOPLIFTER. Behind the times, ain't you?

DAKIS. Yeah, behind the behind.

SHOPLIFTER. (*Feels her pulse.*) Gee, I think I'm getting a reaction. Emotions are bad for me. I got diabetes. I'm not supposed to get emotions.

DAKIS. (*Belches.*) Excuse me. I got ulcers. I'm not supposed to eat sandwiches. A hot meal was waiting for me at home. Do me a favor. Next time get yourself arrested before four o'clock, let a fellow eat a home-cooked meal.

SHOPLIFTER. I'm sorry.

DAKIS. Do you realize this is on my own time? Look at all these forms I had to type up. And when we get to court, what'll happen? The judge'll probably let you off. I won't even get a conviction. You cause me all this work for nothin'.

SHOPLIFTER. I'm sorry . . .

DAKIS. That's a big help.

SHOPLIFTER. I'm sorry . . . (LIEUTENANT *takes address book out of his desk drawer, thumbs through it for a number, reaches for phone, dials.*)

MCLEOD. (*Hangs up. To* GALLANTZ.) Sorry. Nothing yet. We'll follow it up. If we hear anything, we'll let you know.

GALLANTZ. Thanks! My best pants, too. (*He exits* U. L.)

LIEUTENANT. (*On phone.*) Hello. Mrs. McLeod? This is Lieutenant Monoghan at the 21st. No, no! He's all right. Nothing like that! (*The rest of his conversation is drowned out by entrance of* CALLAHAN *with* BARNES *and* BRODY *and* CHARLIE, *all talking at once.* CALLAHAN *and* POLICEMAN *are carrying two suitcases and several pillowcases filled with "loot" from* CHARLIE'S *apartment.* BRODY *completes the parade, carrying in more loot.* CALLAHAN *knocks at* LIEUTENANT'S *door.*) Come in!

DAKIS. How'd you do with Charlie?

CALLAHAN. (*Opens* LIEUTENANT'S *door, holds up "loot."*) Look what we found, boss. And by a strange coincidence—in Charlie's apartment.

BARNES. (*Unlocks* CHARLIE'S *handcuffs.*) Sit down! There! (CHARLIE *sits in designated chair.*)

CALLAHAN. O'Brien is taking Lewis around to identify the houses.

LIEUTENANT. Good! (*Waves him out to squad room.*) Shut the door! (CALLAHAN, *in squad room, aided by* MCLEOD, BRODY *and* DAKIS, *starts dumping stolen goods on table,* U. C. WILLY *enters* U. L. *with suits on hangers, puts them table* U. C.)

CALLAHAN. (*Holding up some loot.*) Look at this! These jockeys sure get around! . . . (LIEUTENANT *picks up his phone and continues conversation, which is drowned out by the racket in squad room as men proceed to help unload stolen goods.* CALLAHAN *holds up an expensive clock, shakes it.*) This worth anything?

MCLEOD. (*Examines it.*) Very good piece. Tiffany. . . . Where'd you get this, Charlie?

CHARLIE. I bought it.

MCLEOD. Where?

CHARLIE. Outside the jewelry exchange. On the street.

BRODY. Who from?

CHARLIE. Some guy ——

MCLEOD. What's his name? (LIEUTENANT *leaves office by door* R.)

CHARLIE. I don't know. I never saw him again.

MCLEOD. Or before?

CHARLIE. (*Nods.*) Yeah.

MCLEOD. Or at all. The little man that wasn't there.

SHOPLIFTER. (*Stands.*) Yeah! I'm getting a reaction. Emotions are bad for me.

DAKIS. (*Checking stolen article against list.*) Girls with diabetes shouldn't steal pink panties.

SHOPLIFTER. It wasn't pink pants.

DAKIS. (*Sighs.*) I know.

SHOPLIFTER. It was a bag.

DAKIS. (*Closes eyes, sighs.*) I know.

SHOPLIFTER. Alligator.

DAKIS. I know.

SHOPLIFTER. Imitation alligator.

DAKIS. (*Sorry he started it all.*) I know.

MCLEOD. Wait! Here's something! Monogrammed: J. G. (*Checks with list.*) Sure. This is some of the Gordon stuff. Where'd you get this, Charlie?

CHARLIE. What's the use of talking? You won't believe me, anyway?

BRODY. Where?

CALLAHAN. Where'd you get it, Charlie? (*Takes out blackjack.*) Know what this is? A persuader. (*Bangs it on desk No.* 2. WILLY *enters* U. L. *Stands by gate.*)

CHARLIE. Go ahead! Beat me! Beat me unconscious. Go ahead.

CALLAHAN. (*Laughs, puts "persuader" away.*) You're too eager, Charlie. Some-a them creeps like it, you know. Gives 'em a thrill. Look at that kisser! I'm a son-of-a-bitch, I'm right!

BRODY. (*Holding up piece of silver.*) Where'd you get this, Charlie? (CHARLIE *hangs his head.*)

DAKIS. Why don't you be professional, Charlie? He's talking to you. . . . What's the matter? What are you hanging your head for? What are you ashamed of? Nobody made you be a burglar. You wanted to be a burglar. So you're a burglar.—So be a good one! Be proud of your chosen profession! Hold your head up. (DAKIS *lifts* CHARLIE'S *head up by the chin.*) That's better. You're a good thief, Charlie. You're no bum. They wear sweaters. Not you!—You got a hundred-dollar suit on. You . . . Wait a minute! (*Opens* CHARLIE'S *coat, looks at label.*) Take it off, you bum. Stolen! The name's still in it. Where'd you get it?

CHARLIE. (*Takes off coat, talking fast.*) You mean it's stolen? O. K. O. K. I'll tell you . . . the whole story . . . may I drop dead on this spot! (DAKIS *hands coat to* BRODY.)

CALLAHAN. On this one? Be careful, Charlie.

CHARLIE. Honest—the truth! But don't tell Lewis!—He'll kill me. He makes out like he's a dummy, don't he? He ain't. He's smart. Ooh, he's as smart as they come. Look . . . I just been in New York two weeks. I came here from Pittsburgh two weeks ago. So help me. I lose my valise in the station. I meet this guy, Lewis, in a poolroom.

CALLAHAN. Where? What poolroom?

CHARLIE. 14th Street, corner of 7th Avenue. . . . Look it up! Check it! I'm telling you the truth, so help me! I shoot a game of pool with him. He says to me, " You got a place to stay? " I says, " No." He says, " Share my flat." I say " O. K." My suit's all dirty. He lends me this one. Says it belongs to his brother, who's in Florida. (*Pause. Looks up at the unbelieving faces circling him.*) So help me!

CALLAHAN. I could tell you a story would bring tears to your eyes. Get in there and take off your pants! (CHARLIE *exits washroom.*)

BRODY. Willy! Got an old pair of pants?

WILLY. Yeah, I got some, somewhere. (*Exits.*)

BRODY. (*To* CHARLIE.) You're not even smart enough to take out the label. The name's still in it. Jerome Armstrong.

CALLAHAN. (*Examining his list.*) Wait! I got that squeal right here. I think there was a rape connected with this one.

BRODY. I wouldn't be surprised.

LIEUTENANT. (*Calls.*) Dakis! (DAKIS *hurries to* LIEUTENANT'S *door, opens it.*)

DAKIS. Yes, sir?

LIEUTENANT. Wait downstairs for Mrs. McLeod. When she gets here, let me know foist.

DAKIS. Right, Chief.

LIEUTENANT. And . . . a . . . Nick! (*Touches his lips.*) Button 'em up.

DAKIS. Yes, sir. (*He goes out* L., *shutting door behind him. As he crossses to gates* U. L. *he glances at* MCLEOD, *his forehead furrows. Exits* U. L. LIEUTENANT *studies his cigar, frowns, goes off* R. *Through the little window we see* CHARLIE *throw up washroom shade, try iron grille-work.* MCLEOD *crosses to washroom door, calls in.*)

MCLEOD. The only way you can get out of there, Charlie, is to jump down the toilet and pull the chain. (JOE FEINSON *enters* U. L. *Comes over to* BRODY.)

JOE. Lot of loot! They do the Zaza robbery?

BRODY. (*To* CHARLIE.) You robbed that Zaza dame's flat, Charlie?

CHARLIE. I don't know nuttin'!

BRODY. He don't know from nuttin'!

CALLAHAN. He's ignorant and he's proud of it.

JOE. Any good names?

BRODY. Don't know yet——

JOE. Any good addresses?

BRODY. They're taking the other bum around. He's identifying the houses. We'll crack this case in an hour. (WILLY *enters* U. L. *with old pants. Gives them to* BRODY, *who throws them to* CHARLIE *in washroom.*)

JOE. (*Saunters over to* MCLEOD.) What's with Schneider?

MCLEOD. No story.

JOE. He left here twenty-five minutes ago in an ambulance. What happened? He trip?

MCLEOD. Yes.

JOE. Over his schnozzola?

MCLEOD. Could have. It's long enough.

JOE. No story?

MCLEOD. No.

JOE. His lawyer's sore as a boil. What happened?

MCLEOD. You tell me. You always have the story in your pocket.

JOE. Look, Seamus! There are angles here I don't feel happy about.

MCLEOD. What angles?

JOE. I don't know . . . yet. Come! Give! Off the record.

MCLEOD. You can print it if you want to. Kurt Schneider was a butcher who murdered two girls and got away with it. High time somebody put the fear of God in him. The law wouldn't, so I did. Print it, Yussel. Go ahead. You don't like the cops. Here's your chance.

JOE. I don't like cops? For a smart guy, Seamus, you can be an awful schmoo. If I got fired tomorrow, you'd still find me here, hanging around, running errands for you guys, happy as a bird dog! I'm a buff way back. I found a home. You know that.

MCLEOD. Sentimental slop, Yussel. (CHARLIE *throws pants out from washroom. They drape on Barnes' neck.* MR. PRITCHETT *enters.*)

JOE. My sixth sense is still bothering me.

MCLEOD. Have a doctor examine it. (*Turning, seeing* PRITCHETT *at gate* U. L.) Yes, sir? (*Recognizes him.*) Oh! Come in, Mr. Pritchett. We've been waiting for you. (JOE *pushes chair* U. S. *end desk No.* 2.)

MR. PRITCHETT. Did you get my money back?

MCLEOD. I'm afraid not.

MR. PRITCHETT. What'd he do with it?

MCLEOD. Women and plush saloons . . . cabarets.

MR. PRITCHETT. Cabarets? I wouldn't have thought it. He seemed such an honest boy. I don't make many mistakes. I'm a pretty good student of human nature! Usually.

MCLEOD. You'll be in court tomorrow morning?

MR. PRITCHETT. Oh, yes.

MCLEOD. We can count on you?

MR. PRITCHETT. When I make my mind up, I'm like iron.

MCLEOD. Fine! Thank you, Mr. Pritchett.

MR. PRITCHETT. Iron.

MCLEOD. Arthur, on your feet! (ARTHUR *rises.*) Is this the boy?

MR. PRITCHETT. I'm afraid it is.

MCLEOD. Arthur, over here. (*Indicating chair below desk No.* 1. ARTHUR *crosses over. Phone rings desk No.* 2—MCLEOD *crosses.*) 21st Squad! McLeod!

BARNES. All right, Charlie. (*Leads* CHARLIE *back into squad room.* CHARLIE *is wearing an ill-fitting, ancient pair of trousers and is disgusted with them.* CHARLIE *sits bench* D. R.)

MR. PRITCHETT. (*Sits* R. *of* ARTHUR.) Well, Arthur, is this your journey's end?

ARTHUR. I guess so.

MR. PRITCHETT. Did I treat you badly?

ARTHUR. No, Mr. Pritchett.

MR. PRITCHETT. Did I pay you a decent salary?

ARTHUR. Yes.

MR. PRITCHETT. Then why did you do this to me? (SUSAN *appears at gate* U. L.)

SUSAN. (*Catches* MCLEOD'S *eyes.*) May I? (*He nods. She comes in, walks across to* ARTHUR *and* MR. PRITCHETT.)

MR. PRITCHETT. (*To* ARTHUR.) You spent my money on fast women?

ARTHUR. Now, just a second . . . !

MR. PRITCHETT. No! I didn't grow my money on trees. I built up my business from a hole in the wall where I sold neckties, two for a quarter. Thirty years I built it. By the sweat of my brow. I worked darn hard for it. I want my money back.

SUSAN. And you'll get it back. I promise you. (*She takes money out of her purse.*) The bank was closed. All I could scrape together tonight, was $120. (*She hands money to* MR. PRITCHETT.) I'll have the rest for you tomorrow.

ARTHUR. Susan! Put that back!

SUSAN. Let me alone! Don't interfere, Jiggs!

MR. PRITCHETT. (*Rises.*) Who is this? Who are you, Miss?

SUSAN. I'm an old friend of Mr. Kindred's family. And I'd like to straighten this out with you. What is your name?

MR. PRITCHETT. Pritchett, Albert J. Pritchett.

SUSAN. Mr. Pritchett. How do you do? I'm Susan Carmichael.

MR. PRITCHETT. How do you do? You say you're prepared to return the rest of my money, young lady?

SUSAN. Yes, I'll sign a promissory note. Or, whatever you suggest.

MCLEOD. (*Into phone.*) One second! (*To* SUSAN.) Where'd you get that cash, Miss Carmichael?

SUSAN. (*Crossing to* MCLEOD.) I had some. And I pawned jewelry. Here are the tickets. Do you want to see them?

MCLEOD. If you don't mind. (*Takes them, examines them.*) Anything of your sister's here?

SUSAN. Nothing. Not a bobby pin.

MR. PRITCHETT. Is this the young lady who . . . ?

ARTHUR. No. She doesn't know anything about it.

SUSAN. I know all there is to know. (*To* MR. PRITCHETT.) Mr. Pritchett, this whole mess you can blame on my sister.

ARTHUR. What's the matter with you, Suzy? What are you dragging Joy into this for? She's got nothing to do with it.

SUSAN. (*Crossing* D. L.) Hasn't she?

ARTHUR. No.

SUSAN. I've got news for you. I just spoke to her on the phone. (*Pause.*)

ARTHUR. You didn't tell her?

SUSAN. Of course I did.

ARTHUR. What'd she say?

SUSAN. She was upset.

ARTHUR. Naturally, she would be. You shouldn't have . . .

SUSAN. Naturally? My blue-eyed sister was in a tizzy because she didn't want to get involved in your troubles. You know where I called her? At Walter Forbes' in Connecticut. She's afraid this might crimp her chances to be the next Mrs. Forbes. . . . Big deal!

ARTHUR. I know, Suzy. That's not news to me. I know.

SUSAN. Till ten minutes ago, I thought my sister was the Cherubim of the world. There wasn't anything I wouldn't have done for her. But if she can do this to you—to you, Jiggs—then I don't want any part of her. And I mean that. I'm through with her. I loathe her.

ARTHUR. Suzy! Take it easy.

SUSAN. All my life everything I wanted Joy got. All right! I didn't mind. I felt she was so special. She was entitled to be Queen. But now I'm through.

ARTHUR. Suzy, maybe you don't understand? Like everybody else, Joy is frightened. She wants to grab a little security. Don't blame her for it. I don't.

SUSAN. Security? You've seen Walter Forbes. He's had four wives. He gets falling-down drunk every single night of his life. Some security!

ARTHUR. (*Crossing to chair, sits.*) He's very rich. You can't have everything.

SUSAN. Jiggs! Don't! Don't you be disgusting, too. (*To* MR. PRITCHETT.) Should I make out a note for the rest?

MCLEOD. Wait a minute. (*Hangs up phone, crosses to* MR. PRITCHETT, *takes money from him, hands it back to* SUSAN.) We don't run a collection agency here! This man is a thief. We're here to prosecute criminals, not collect money. (DAKIS *comes in* U. L., *crosses into* LIEUTENANT'S *office, pantomimes to* LIEUTENANT *off* R.: MRS. MCLEOD *is downstairs. Exits* U. L.)

SUSAN. He's not a criminal.

MCLEOD. Miss Carmichael, you seem like a very nice young lady. I'm going to give you some advice. I've seen a thousand like him. *He's no good!* Take your money and run.

LIEUTENANT. (*Comes out of office, calls* MCLEOD.) McLeod!

MCLEOD. (*Crosses toward him.*) Yes, sir!

LIEUTENANT Get me the old files on the Cottsworth squeal!

MCLEOD. (*Thinks.*) 1938?

LIEUTENANT. Yeah.

MCLEOD. March 12th . . . (LIEUTENANT *nods.*) That'll be buried under a pile inside. I'll have to dig them up.

LIEUTENANT. Dig 'em up! Do it now!

MCLEOD. Yes, sir. (*As he crosses off* D. L.) He spells one thing for you—*misery* the rest of your life. He's no good. Believe me, I know! (*Exits* D. L.)

SUSAN. (*Indignantly.*) That isn't true! (*To* MR. PRITCHETT.) That isn't true. I've known Arthur all my life. He never did a thing before in his life that was dishonorable. He was the most respected boy in Ann Arbor. (BRODY *crosses down to listen to* SUSAN *and* MR. PRITCHETT.)

MR. PRITCHETT. Little lady, once I saw a picture, LESS MISERABLES.—A dandy! That was before your time. This Gene Valjeane—his sister's nine children are starving. He steals a loaf of bread. He goes to jail for—I don't know—twenty years. I'm on Gene Valjeane's side there. Impressed me very much. I gave a little talk on it at my lodge. . . . But this? I don't go along with. He wasn't starving. He had a good job. He went cabareting . . . With my money? Heck, I don't go to them myself!

BRODY. Mr. Pritchett, maybe once a year we get someone in here steals because he's actually hungry. And we're all on his side. I'd do the same, wouldn't you?

MR. PRITCHETT. Absolutely. I always say self-preservation is the first law of nature.

BRODY. But that's one in a thousand cases.

MR. PRITCHETT. Exactly my point! And what did *he* do it for?

ARTHUR. (*Softly.*) I did it because I was hungry.

MR. PRITCHETT. What?

ARTHUR. Hungry. You can be hungry for other things besides bread. You've been decent to me, Mr. Pritchett. You trusted me, and I let you down. I'm sorry. It's hard to explain, even to myself. I'd been separated from my girl for five years,—five long, bloody years! The one human being in the world I loved. She's very beautiful, Mr. Pritchett. Tall, a silvery blond girl . . . Warm, understanding.

SUSAN. Jiggs, don't!

ARTHUR. At least she was. She was, Susan. We all change. When I came back from the war, I tried going back to school, but I couldn't get myself settled. I came to New York just to be near her. She'd moved on into a new world. She was out of my reach. I should have accepted that. I couldn't. To take her out to dinner and hold her hand cost a month's salary. I hung on, anyway. Last Wednesday I had to face it. I was going to lose my girl. She told me she wanted to marry someone else. I made a final grandstand play for her. Late collections had come in. Your money was in my pocket. I blew the works on her. I didn't give a damn about anything except holding on to her. It was my last chance. I lost, anyway . . .

BRODY. You admit you did wrong?

ARTHUR. Yes, God, yes!

BRODY. You're willing to make restitution?

ARTHUR. If I get the chance.

SUSAN. Tomorrow morning. I promise you!

BRODY. That's in his favor. How do you feel, Mr. Pritchett?

MR. PRITCHETT. Well. . . .

BRODY. This kid has a fine war record, too, remember.

MR. PRITCHETT. I know.

BRODY. He took a lot of chances for us, maybe we ought to take one for him. You see, these kids got problems nobody ever had. We don't even understand them. New blood. We're varicosed. I guess if a new world is gonna be made, looks like they're the ones gotta do it.

MR. PRITCHETT. It's funny you should say that. I was talking to my brother-in-law only the other night about my nephew and I made exactly that point. I was saying to him . . .

BRODY. Mr. Pritchett, do you mind stepping over here a minute?

MR. PRITCHETT. Not at all! (*Rises, follows him to files* D. L.)

BRODY. You, too, Miss!

CHARLIE. Give me another cigarette.

BARNES. What do you do? Eat these things?

CHARLIE. Give me a cigarette! (BARNES *gives him another cigarette.* DAKIS *enters* U. L., *with* MRS. MCLEOD, *leads her to* LIEUTENANT'S *office.*)

JOE. How do you do, Mrs. McLeod! Remember me? I'm Joe Feinson, the reporter.

MARY. (*Studies him for a split second, then recalls him.*) Oh, yes, of course. I met you with my husband. What's happened to Jim?
JOE. Nothing. He's all right. He's in there.
MARY. Mr. Feinson, please tell me!
JOE. I am.
DAKIS. (*Holds door open.*) This way, please. . . . (*She follows him into* LIEUTENANT'S *office.* DAKIS *sits desk No.* 2. JOE *exits* U. L. CALLAHAN *crosses and sits desk No. 1.*)
LIEUTENANT. How do you do, Mrs. McLeod?
MARY. Lieutenant Monoghan?
LIEUTENANT. Yes, ma'm.
MARY. What is this about, Lieutenant?
LIEUTENANT. Have a seat?
MARY. Where's my husband?
LIEUTENANT. He'll be back in a few minutes.
MARY. He hasn't been *shot?*
LIEUTENANT. No-o-o!
MARY. I had a terrible feeling that he . . .
LIEUTENANT. Nothing like that. He's all right.
MARY. You're sure? You're not trying to break it easy?
LIEUTENANT. Nothing like that! I give you my word. You'll see him in a few minutes.
MARY. Then what is it? What's wrong?
LIEUTENANT. A certain situation has come up, and you might be able to help us out.
MARY. Me? . . . I'm all at sea, Lieutenant!
LIEUTENANT. Mrs. McLeod, your husband and I never got along too well, I want you to know that right now I'm sticking my neck out a mile to save him. I'm not doing it because I like him—I don't. I'm doing it because he has a value here and I need him on the squad. So, like I say, I'm going to help him, if you help me.
MARY. What kind of trouble is Jim in?
LIEUTENANT. (*Crossing around desk, sits.*) A prisoner here was assaulted, maybe injured by your husband.
MARY. Jim wouldn't do that.
LIEUTENANT. He did. You'll have to take my word for it.
MARY. Then there must have been a reason. A very good reason.
LIEUTENANT. That's what I have to find out.

MARY. Jim is kind and gentle.
LIEUTENANT. That's one side of him.
MARY. It's the only side I know. I've never seen any other.
LIEUTENANT. Please sit down!
MARY. Is this man badly hurt?
LIEUTENANT. I don't know yet. This could become serious, Mrs. McLeod. This might cost your husband his job. He could even wind up in jail.
MARY. (*Sinks into chair* L. *of desk.*) How can I help?
LIEUTENANT. By answering some questions. By telling me the truth. Are you willing to go along?
MARY. Yes, of course.
LIEUTENANT. Did you ever run into a man named Kurt Schneider?
MARY. (*Hoarsely.*) No. (*Coughs.*)
LIEUTENANT. My cigar bothering you?
MARY. No. I love the smell of a cigar. My father always smoked them.
LIEUTENANT. Did you ever hear your husband mention that name?
MARY. What name?
LIEUTENANT. This prisoner's name? Kurt Schneider.
MARY. (*Shakes head.*) Jim made it a rule never to discuss his work with me.
LIEUTENANT. It's a good rule. We don't like to bring this sordid stuff into our homes.
MARY. I'm well trained now. I don't ask.
LIEUTENANT. How long you been married?
MARY. Three years.
LIEUTENANT. It took me ten years to train my wife. It's a tough life—being married to a cop.
MARY. I don't think so. I'm happy.
LIEUTENANT. You love your husband?
MARY. Very much.
LIEUTENANT. Where did you live before you were married? (*Phone in squad room rings desk No.* 2.)
DAKIS. (*Answers phone.*) 21st Squad, Detective Dakis.
MARY. New York.
LIEUTENANT. You don't sound like a native. Where you from? Upstate?
MARY. Highland Falls. You've got a good ear.

LIEUTENANT. It's my business.

DAKIS. (*Knocks on* LIEUTENANT'S *door.*) Captain on the phone, Lieutenant. (*Returns to desk No.* 2.)

LIEUTENANT. Excuse me! . . . (*Picks up phone. In squad room* SHOPLIFTER *rises and stretches.*)

SHOPLIFTER. (*To* CALLAHAN, *who is at desk No.* 1 *typing.*) You don't look like a detective.

CALLAHAN. No? What does a detective look like?

SHOPLIFTER. They wear derbies. (*She giggles.*) You're a nice-looking fellow.

CALLAHAN. Thanks.

SHOPLIFTER. Are you married?

CALLAHAN. Yes.

SHOPLIFTER. (*Disgusted—the story of her life.*) Ya-a-a! (*Sits down again above desk No.* 1.)

LIEUTENANT. Thanks, Captain! (*Hangs up, turns to* MRS. MCLEOD.) When'd you leave Highland Falls?

MARY. The spring of 1941. I got a job in a defense plant.

LIEUTENANT. Where?

MARY. In Newark.

LIEUTENANT. (*Rises, crosses* U. S.) This doctor was practicing in Newark about that time.

MARY. Doctor?

LIEUTENANT. Schneider.

MARY. Oh, he's a doctor?

LIEUTENANT. Yes. You never met him? Around Newark, maybe?

MARY. No. I don't know him.

LIEUTENANT. (*Sits on desk No.* 3.) He knows you.

MARY. What makes you think that?

LIEUTENANT. He said so.

MARY. I'm afraid he's mistaken.

LIEUTENANT. He was positive. . . . Kurt Schneider! Ring any bells?

MARY. No. I'm afraid not.

LIEUTENANT. You averted my gaze then. Why?

MARY. Did I? I wasn't conscious of it.

LIEUTENANT. Are you sure a Dr. Schneider never treated you?

MARY. (*Indignantly.*) Certainly not. I just told you: "No."

LIEUTENANT. Why are you so indignant? I didn't say what he treated you for.

MARY. Did this man tell my husband he treated me?

LIEUTENANT. (*Sits desk No. 3,* U. S.) If you'll tell the truth, Mrs. McLeod, you'll help your husband. You'll save me time and trouble. But that's all. In the end, I'll get the correct answers. We got a hundred ways of finding out the truth.

MARY. I don't know what you're talking about, Lieutenant. I'm not lying. (GALLAGHER *arrives* U. L. *with* TAMI GIACOPPETTI, *a handsome, swarthy man, very expensively dressed.*)

GALLAGHER. One second, Tami.

GIACOPPETTI. Can I use the phone, Champ?

GALLAGHER. Not yet, Tami. (*Knocks at* LIEUTENANT'S *door.*)

GIACOPPETTI. (*Stands* U. C.) O. K., Champ.

LIEUTENANT. Yeah! (GALLAGHER *hands note to* LIEUTENANT, *who glances at it, pockets it.*) Mrs. McLeod, I'm going to ask you a very personal question. Don't get angry. I would never dream of asking any woman this type of question unless I had to. You must regard me as the impersonal voice of the law. Mrs. McLeod, did Dr. Schneider ever perform an abortion on you?

MARY. (*Rising.*) You've no right to ask me that!

LIEUTENANT. I have to do my job—and my job is to find out the truth. Let's not waste any more time! Please answer that question!

MARY. It seems to me I have some rights to privacy. My past life concerns nobody but me.

LIEUTENANT. You have the right to tell the truth. Did he?

MARY. No, Lieutenant Monoghan, he did not.

LIEUTENANT. Does this name mean anything to you? Tami Giacoppetti?

MARY. No. (LIEUTENANT *opens door to squad room, and calls:*)

LIEUTENANT. Mr. Giacoppetti! (TAMI *enters* LIEUTENANT'S *office, sees* MARY, *crosses down to her.*)

GIACOPPETTI. (*Very softly.*) Hello, Mary. (*She withers, all evasion gone, her head droops as she avoids their glance.*)

LIEUTENANT. (*To* MARY.) Would you mind stepping in here a minute! (*Indicating room off* R. *They exit* R. TAMI *sits* L. *of desk No. 3. Whistling a tune,* O'BRIEN *returns with* LEWIS *and* KEOGH.)

BARNES. Here's your boy friend, Charlie!

DAKIS. (*Rises, crossing* D. L.) How'd you do?

O'BRIEN. We got the addresses and most of the names.

DAKIS. How many?

O'BRIEN. Nine. (*To* LEWIS.) Sit down! Over here! Lewis has been very cooperative. (LEWIS *sits above desk No.* 2.)
CALLAHAN. Whither to, Charlie?
CHARLIE. I got to go.
CALLAHAN. Again? This makes the sixth time.
CHARLIE. Well, I'm noivous.
BARNES. Sit down, Charlie! (CHARLIE *sits bench down* R.)
CALLAHAN. He's noivous, poor kid.
O'BRIEN. He needs a vacation.
DAKIS. He's gonna get one. A long one. At the State's expense. (*Sits, No. 1 desk.*)
CALLAHAN. (*Seated* L. *of desk No.* 2.) Nuttin's too good for Charlie. (*Dialing on phone. On phone.*) Hello, Mrs. Lundstrom? This is Detective Callahan of the Twenty-foist Squad. We got that property was burglarized from your apartment. Will you please come down and identify it? Yeah! Yeah! We got 'em. Right. Yes, ma'am. (*Hangs up, looks at squeal card, dials another number.*)
O'BRIEN. (*On phone, desk No.* 2, *simultaneously.*) Hello, Mr. Donatello, please. Mr. Donatello? This is Detective O'Brien of the 21st Squad. Yes, sir. I think we've caught them. Yes. I have some articles here. Not all. Would you mind coming down to the station house and identifying them? Right. (*Hangs up.*)
CALLAHAN. (*On phone.*) Hello! Mrs. Demetrios? This is Detective Callahan. Remember me? Twenty-foist Squad. Yeah. I'm still roarin'! How are you, Toots? (*Laughs.*) Return match? Where's your husband, tonight? Okay. (MCLEOD *enters from door* D. L. *with bundle of records wrapped in a sheet of dusty paper, tied with twine.*) I'll be off duty after midnight. Oh, by the way, we got that stuff was burglarized from your apartment. Come down and identify it. O. K., yuh barracuda! (*Hangs up.*) A man-eater.
O'BRIEN. You watch it!
CALLAHAN. What I don't do for the good of the soivice! I should be getting foist-grade money.
MCLEOD. (*Undoing package.*) You'll be getting a "foist" grade knock on the head.
CALLAHAN. (*Disdainfully.*) Brain trust. (*Walks away* U. R.)
BRODY. (*To* MCLEOD, C.) Say, Jim. I had a long talk with Mr. Pritchett and he's willing to drop the charges.
MCLEOD. He is? (*Crosses over to them.*) What's this about, Mr. Pritchett?

MR. PRITCHETT. I decided not to bring charges against . . . (*Nods to* ARTHUR.)

MCLEOD. I thought you were going to go through with this?

MR. PRITCHETT. I'd like to give the boy another chance.

MCLEOD. To steal from someone else?

MR. PRITCHETT. I wouldn't want this on my conscience.

MCLEOD. Supposing he commits a worse crime. What about your conscience then, Mr. Pritchett?

MR. PRITCHETT. I'll gamble—I'm a gambler. I bet on horses. This once I'll bet on a human being.

MCLEOD. Stick to horses—the percentage is better.

BRODY. Wait a minute, Jim. I advised Mr. Pritchett to do this. I thought . . .

MCLEOD. (*Harshly.*) You had no right to do that, Lou. This is my case. You know better.

BRODY. I didn't think you'd mind.

MCLEOD. Well, I do.

BRODY. (*Angrily.*) Well, I'm sorry! (KEOGH *enters* U. L.)

SUSAN. But I'm going to return the money. And if he's satisfied, what difference does it make to you?

MCLEOD. It isn't as easy as that. This isn't a civil action. This is a *criminal* action.

GUS. (*Enters with sheet in his hand.*) Jim! Look at this sheet on Charlie! As long as your arm. (MCLEOD *takes it, studies it.* GUS *to* BARNES.) You better keep your eye on that son-of-a-bitch! (MCLEOD *still studying sheet, exits with* O'BRIEN *through gate* U. L.)

MR. PRITCHETT. (*To* BRODY.) But you said . . . ?

BRODY. I'm sorry. I made a mistake. It's his case. The disposition of it is up to him.

SUSAN. But if everybody concerned is . . .

BRODY. I'm sorry, girlie. You gotta leave me outa this. I got no right to interfere. Take it up with him. (*Walks away off* L., *out door* D. L., *leaving* SUSAN *and* PRITCHETT *suspended in mid-air.* SUSAN *sinks into chair* R. *of desk No. 1, waits for* MCLEOD'S *return, glancing off despairingly in his direction.* LIEUTENANT *returns to his office from anteroom.*)

GIACOPPETTI. (*Rises.*) What's this about, Champ?

LIEUTENANT. Sit down, Tami! (*Picks up* TAMI'S *hat, which is on desk No. 3, looks at label in it.*) Dobbs Beaver? (*Impressed.*) A twenty-buck hat. You must be rolling.

GIACOPPETTI. (*Sits* L. *of desk No. 3.*) Forty bucks. I'm comfortable. No complaints. What's on your mind, Champ?

LIEUTENANT. (*Sits in swivel chair.*) The woman you just said hello to.

GIACOPPETTI. Mary! What kind of trouble could she be in?

LIEUTENANT. I'd just like a little information.

GIACOPPETTI. (*Frowns.*) That girl's a hundred-per-cent. I wouldn't say a word against her.

LIEUTENANT. You don't have to. She ain't in no trouble.

GIACOPPETTI. No? That's good. What do you want from me, Champ?

LIEUTENANT. Mr. Giacoppetti, all this is off the record.

GIACOPPETTI. When I talk, it's always for the record, Champ. I only say something when I got something to say, Champ.

LIEUTENANT. Look, Giacoppetti, I'm Lieutenant Monoghan. I'm in charge here. Keep your tongue in your mouth, and we'll get along.

GIACOPPETTI. Mind if I phone my lawyer?

LIEUTENANT. It ain't necessary.

GIACOPPETTI. My lawyer gets mad.

LIEUTENANT. Nothing you say here will be held against you, understand? I give you my woid.

GIACOPPETTI. I won't hurt that girl.

LIEUTENANT. I don't want you to. She's only a witness. It's someone else.

GIACOPPETTI. O. K. Shoot!

LIEUTENANT. Married?

GIACOPPETTI. Yeah.

LIEUTENANT. How long?

GIACOPPETTI. Fifteen years. What a racket that is!

LIEUTENANT. You're an expert, ain't you?

GIACOPPETTI. On what? Marriage?

LIEUTENANT. Rackets.

GIACOPPETTI. I'm a legitimate business man. Take it up with my attorney.

LIEUTENANT. Look, Mr. Giacoppetti. We've got a sheet on you. We know you're in black market up to your neck. But we don't operate in the State of New Jersey. And what went on there ain't none of our business. Unless you make it so. Kapish?

GIACOPPETTI. Yeah, I kapish.
LIEUTENANT. Got any kids?
GIACOPPETTI. No.
LIEUTENANT. I got five. You don't know what you're missing, Tami.
GIACOPPETTI. (*Rises, furious.*) Don't rub salt in! I know. I got a wife as big as the Sahara Desert—and twice as sterile. I got nine brothers, four sisters . . . all on my payroll. None of 'em worth anything. They got kids—like rabbits they got 'em—nephews, nieces all over the lot. But a guy like me, I should become a nation, and I got no kids. (*Crosses* D. L.) Not one. So don't rub salt in, eh?
LIEUTENANT. (*Laughs.*) O. K. I guess I know how you feel.
GIACOPPETTI. (*Controls himself, smiles sheepishly.*) You're a sharpshooter, Champ. You hit me right on my spot.
LIEUTENANT. When did you know this girl?
GIACOPPETTI. Seven years ago.
LIEUTENANT. You like her?
GIACOPPETTI. (*Crosses* L.) I was crazy about her. She was my girl once. I'd married her if I could have gotten a divorce.
LIEUTENANT. What broke it up?
GIACOPPETTI. I don't know.
LIEUTENANT. What do you think?
GIACOPPETTI. (*Crosses to desk.*) I think maybe I better call my lawyer.
LIEUTENANT. Come on, Giacoppetti. What the hell! You've gone this far. It's off the record. Gave you my woid.
GIACOPPETTI. Aah, she gave me the air! She got caught . . . and that soured her on me. Dames! Who can understand them?
LIEUTENANT. Send her to a doctor?
GIACOPPETTI. To a doctor? Me? I wanted that kid. I told her: " Give me a son—anything goes." Anything she wants. The moon out of the sky . . . I'd get it for her. Dames! Who can understand them? She goes off. That's the last I see of her. Next thing I know I hear she went to some doctor. I went looking for her. If I'd 'a' found her, I'd 'a' broken her neck. I found him, though. I personally beat the hell out of him. Sent him to a hospital.
LIEUTENANT. What was his name?
GIACOPPETTI. A Dutchman. Schneider . . . something.
LIEUTENANT. Kurt Schneider.

GIACOPPETTI. That's it. (LIEUTENANT *goes toward door* R., *beckons* MARY *in.*)

LIEUTENANT. Thank you, Tami!

GIACOPPETTI. That all?

LIEUTENANT. Almost.

GIACOPPETTI. Now will you tell me what this is about, Champ?

LIEUTENANT. Just a minute. (MARY *enters.*) Mrs. McLeod, Mr. Giacoppetti has told me everything.

MARY. He has?

GIACOPPETTI. In a case like this, they find out, anyway. It's better to. (MARY *folds up, begins to weep.*)

LIEUTENANT. I'm sorry, Mrs. McLeod. (*To* GIACOPPETTI.) Mr. Giacoppetti! (*Beckons him, both exit off* R.)

MCLEOD. (*As it is getting dark in squad room,* MCLEOD *re-enters,* U. L., CHARLIE'S *sheet in his hand.*) So you didn't done it, Charlie. (*Switches on lights.*)

CHARLIE. (*Weeping.*) No! No! On my mother's grave!

MCLEOD. And you never been in jail?

CHARLIE. (*Wailing.*) May I drop dead on this spot! What do you guys want from me?

MCLEOD. (*To* MR. PRITCHETT.) Heartbreaking, isn't it? (*Crosses to* CHARLIE.) These are your fingerprints, Charlie. They never lie. (*Reads sheet. Crosses* D. *to* CHARLIE *on bench.*) Burglary, eight arrests. Five assaults. Seven muggings. Three rapes. Six extortions. Three jail sentences. One prison break! Twenty-seven arrests. Nice little sheet, Charlie. This bum is a four-time loser. You have a club. If he makes one false move—you know what to do with it—hit him over the head.

BARNES. Don't worry, I will.

MCLEOD. Book him! Book this bum, too! (*Nods in* LEWIS' *direction.* LEWIS *rises.*)

CHARLIE. (*Looks at* MCLEOD.) Hey, got a cigarette?

MCLEOD. What do you want—room service?

CHARLIE. It's the green-light hotel, ain't it?

MCLEOD. (*Growls.*) Take him away!

BARNES. O. K. Charlie, come on. (*Exit* BARNES, *and* CHARLIE, U. L., *laughing his head off at* MCLEOD.)

MCLEOD. (*Turns to* MR. PRITCHETT.) Don't invest these criminals with your nervous system, Mr. Pritchett. Sure! They laugh, they cry. But don't think it's your laughter or your tears. It isn't.

They're a different species, a different breed. Believe me, I know. I know it from my childhood. (JOE FEINSON *enters* U. L., *stands at gate.*)

SUSAN. My God—didn't you ever make a mistake?

MCLEOD. Yes. When I was new on this job we brought in two boys who were caught stealing from a car. They looked like babies. They cried. I let them go. Two nights later—two nights later—one of them held up a butcher in Harlem. Shot him through the head an' killed him. Yes, I made a mistake, and I'm not going to do it again.

SUSAN. But, Officer, you . . .

MCLEOD. (*Harshly.*) Young lady, I don't want to discuss this with you. Now don't interrupt me again.

ARTHUR. (*Rises.*) Don't talk to her like that. She has a right to speak.

MCLEOD. (*Roars at* ARTHUR.) Shut up! Sit down! (ARTHUR *sits.* MCLEOD *controls himself, lights cigarette.*) When you're dealing with the criminal mind, Mr. Pritchett, softness is dangerous.

MR. PRITCHETT. But if it's a first offense?

MCLEOD. It's never a first offense! It's just the first time they get caught.

SUSAN. Why are you so vicious?

MCLEOD. I'm not vicious, young lady. I didn't steal this man's money. (*Extinguishes match, hurls it in* ARTHUR'S *direction.*) He did. (*To* MR. PRITCHETT; *crosses* D. C.) This is a war, Mr. Pritchett. We know it; they know it; but you don't. We're your army. We're here to protect you. But you've got to cooperate. I'm sick and tired of massaging the complainant into doing his simple duty. You civilians are too lazy or too selfish or too scared or just too indifferent to even want to appear in court and see the charges through that you, yourselves, bring. That makes us—street-cleaners. They have a stick, sweep out the streets; we have a stick—sweep out the human garbage; they pile it in wagons, dump it in the East River; we pile it in wagons, dump it in the Tombs. And what happens?—The next day . . . all back again.

MR. PRITCHETT. But if I get paid . . .

MCLEOD. I don't care about that. This is a criminal action. Are you? Or aren't you? Because I'm not going to let this go.

MR. PRITCHETT. If I don't bring charges?

MCLEOD. Then I'm going to book him, anyway, and subpoena you into court.

MR. PRITCHETT. Well . . . I . . . I . . .

MCLEOD. It's my duty to protect you in spite of yourself.

MR. PRITCHETT. I guess I've got to leave it up to you, Officer. Whatever you say.

MCLEOD. (*Crossing to* MR. PRITCHETT.) I say prosecute.

MR. PRITCHETT. All right! You know best. (*To* SUSAN.) I'm sorry. But he had no right to rob me . . . in the first place . . . that was a terrible thing to do.

MCLEOD. (*Takes him by arm, leads him toward gate.*) We won't take up any more of your time. In court tomorrow morning at ten. (MR. PRITCHETT *exits* U. L.)

SUSAN. Mister Pritchett . . . (*Runs after him and off* U. L.)

MCLEOD. There goes John Q. Public. " A man of iron! "

JOE. Humble yourself, sweetheart! Humble yourself!

MCLEOD. What?

JOE. Seamus, Seamus, why must you always make everything so black and white? Remember, we're all of us falling down all the time. Don't be so intolerant.

MCLEOD. You're out of line.

JOE. Listen to me, Seamus. Listen! I love you, and I'm trying to warn you.

MCLEOD. What about? What's on your mind?

JOE. You're digging your own grave. It's right there in front of you. One more step and you're in. Now humble yourself, sweetheart, humble yourself!

MCLEOD. You're very Delphic today, Yussel. What's the oracle of C. C. N. Y. trying to tell me?

JOE. Nothing. Forget it. (*He goes* U. L.)

LIEUTENANT. (*Returns to his office, followed by* GIACOPPETTI. MARY *rises.*) You feel better?

MARY. Yes. Thank you.

LIEUTENANT. Are you ready to tell me the truth?

MARY. Yes.

LIEUTENANT. Your husband's been after Schneider a long time because of this?

MARY. No.

LIEUTENANT. Schneider's attorney says so.

MARY. I don't care what he says. Jim never knew. He never knew. I'm sure of that.

LIEUTENANT. Careful now! Weigh your words. This is very important. Any minute that phone'll ring. If Schneider is critically hurt, it's out of my hands. The next second this case'll be with the homicide squad. The Commissioner'll be here, the District Attorney. If that happens, I gotta have all the facts.

MARY. Jim didn't know.

LIEUTENANT. That's the question I gotta be sure of . . . now. (*Calls:*) McLeod!

MCLEOD. Yes, sir? (MCLEOD *enters* LIEUTENANT'S *office, sees* MARY, *stops short.*) Mary! What are you doing here? What's this, Lieutenant? What's my wife . . . ?

LIEUTENANT. I sent for her.

MCLEOD. Why?

LIEUTENANT. This is Mr. Giacoppetti.

GIACOPPETTI. Hi, Champ!

MCLEOD. What's this about, Lieutenant?

LIEUTENANT. Schneider! Why'd you lie to me?

MCLEOD. I didn't lie to you.

MARY. May I . . . may I . . . please?

LIEUTENANT. Yes. Go ahead. (*Watching* MCLEOD.)

MARY. Jim, the Lieutenant won't believe me that you knew nothing about this . . . I . . .

MCLEOD. About what, Mary?

MARY. Dr. Schneider.

MCLEOD. What's he got to do with you?

MARY. This man you struck, this Dr. Schneider . . .

MCLEOD. Don't keep saying that, Mary. He's no doctor.

MARY. He isn't? I thought he was. I . . . had occasion to see him once. I went to him once when I needed help.

MCLEOD. You what?

MARY. A long time ago, Jim. (*To* LIEUTENANT.) I told you he didn't . . .

MCLEOD. Wait a minute! What's he got to do with this?

MARY. We were going together.

MCLEOD. I see.

MARY. I . . .

MCLEOD. O. K. Diagrams aren't necessary. I get the picture.

GIACOPPETTI. I beat the hell out of this Schneider myself.

(*Touches* MCLEOD *on arm.* MCLEOD, *with a roar, slaps his hand.*) Geeze! (*Holds his hand in agony.*)

LIEUTENANT. Cut that out!

GIACOPPETTI. I don't have to take that from you, Champ!

MCLEOD. Touch me again and I'll tear your arm out of the socket.

LIEUTENANT. (*To* MCLEOD.) You cut that out! In one second I'm going to flatten you myself. (*Pause.*)

MCLEOD. Do you mind if I talk to my wife . . . alone? (LIEUTENANT *looks at* MARY.)

MARY. Please!

LIEUTENANT. All right, Tami. You can go. (GIACOPPETTI *goes through squad room off* U. L. LIEUTENANT *walks into his anteroom* U. R., *slams door.*)

MARY. I'm terribly sorry, Jim. Please forgive me. (*She touches him. He moves away to avoid her touch.*) Is this man badly hurt?

MCLEOD. No.

MARY. Then you're not in serious trouble, Jim?

MCLEOD. He's only acting. Nothing will come of it.

MARY. You're sure?

MCLEOD. Yes.

MARY. Thank God for that.

MCLEOD. My immaculate wife!

MARY. I never said I was.

MCLEOD. You never said you weren't! Why didn't you tell me?

MARY. I loved you and I was afraid of losing you.

MCLEOD. How long did you go with him?

MARY. A few months.

MCLEOD. How many?

MARY. About four.

MCLEOD. Four isn't a few.

MARY. No, I suppose not.

MCLEOD. Did he give you money?

MARY. No.

MCLEOD. But he did give you presents?

MARY. Yes. He gave me some presents, of course.

MCLEOD. Expensive ones?

MARY. I don't know.

MCLEOD. What do you mean you don't know?

MARY. I don't know. What difference does it make?

MCLEOD. This difference. I'd just as soon Schneider died. I'd sooner go to jail for twenty years—than find out this way that my wife was a whore.

MARY. Don't say that, Jim.

MCLEOD. That's the word. I didn't invent it. That's what they call it.

MARY. I don't care what anybody says. I only care about you, Jim, and it isn't true. You know it isn't true.

MCLEOD. Why didn't you tell me?

MARY. I wanted to, but I didn't dare. I would have lost you.

MCLEOD. I thought I knew you. I thought you were everything good and pure. . . . And with a pig like that! Live dirt!

MARY. Jim, don't judge me. Try and understand. Right and wrong aren't always as simple as they seem to you. I was on my own for the first time in a large city. The war was on. Everything was feverish! I'd only been out with kids my own age until I met this man. He paid me a lot of attention. I was flattered. I'd never met anyone like him before in my whole life. I thought he was romantic and glamorous. I thought I was in love with him. (*Phone on desk No. 2 rings in squad room.*)

MCLEOD. Are you trying to justify yourself in those terms?

MARY. Not justify! Just explain. It was wrong. I know it. I discovered that for myself.

MCLEOD. When? Just now?

MARY. Jim, I'm trying to make my life everything you want it to be. If I could make my past life over I'd do that, too, gladly. But I can't. No one can. I made a mistake. I admit it. I've paid for it . . . plenty. Isn't that enough?

DAKIS. (*Crosses to* LIEUTENANT'S *office, opens door, looks in.*) Where's the Lieutenant?

MCLEOD. Inside.

DAKIS. (*Shouting, off.*) Lieutenant!—Hospital's on the phone.

LIEUTENANT. (*Enters, picks up phone on desk No. 3.*) Lieutenant Monoghan—21st. . . . Yeah! . . . Put him on! . . . Yeah? You're sure? O. K., Doc. Thank you. (*Hangs up.*) The devil takes care of his own! . . . It looks like Schneider is all right. They can't find anything wrong with him. (*A pause.*)

MARY. May I go now?

LIEUTENANT. Yes, Mrs. McLeod. (*Exit* LIEUTENANT *off* R.)

MARY. Jim, I beg you! Please understand.

MCLEOD. What's there to understand? . . . You got undressed before him.

MARY. Jim!

MCLEOD. You went to bed with him.

MARY. Jim! I can't take much more of this.

MCLEOD. You carried his child awhile inside you . . . and then you killed it.

MARY. Yes. That's true.

MCLEOD. Everything I hate . . . even murder. . . . What the hell's left to understand! (MARY *backs up to door of* LIEUTENANT'S *office, opens it, turns, flees,* U. L. *and off.*)

CURTAIN

ACT III

Set clock at 8:35.

MCLEOD *is seated at typewriter on desk No. 1,* ARTHUR *in a chair near desk No. 1;* SUSAN *stands behind* ARTHUR'S *chair,* SHOPLIFTER *sits in chair above desk No. 1,* BRODY L. *of fingerprint board, with* LEWIS *at* R. *of it,* MR. AND MRS. BAGATELLE *are behind rail at door* U. L.; CALLAHAN *at gate talking with them as they leave. They do soon after curtain has risen,* LADY *and* GENTLEMAN *are talking with* KEOGH *between desk No. 2 and gate,* DAKIS *is at up-stage edge of desk No. 2,* JOE *is below desk No. 2, his foot on chair as he watches* LADY *and* GENTLEMAN; PHOTOGRAPHER *squats down* L. C., *back to footlights,* CHARLIE *seated at downstage end of bench down* R.; BARNES *standing at upstage end of same bench. As curtain rises,* CALLAHAN *goes to chair* R. *of desk No. 2, and sits.*

PHOTOGRAPHER. (D. L. *to chic* LADY, *who holds stolen silver tureen.*) Hold up the loot! Little higher, please! (*She holds it higher. Flash!*)
MCLEOD. (*At desk No. 1 to* ARTHUR.) Hair?
ARTHUR. Brown.
MCLEOD. Eyes?
ARTHUR. Eyes? I don't know . . . greenish?
MCLEOD. (*Peering at* ARTHUR.) Look brown.
SUSAN. Hazel. Brown and green flecked with gold.
MCLEOD. Hazel. (*Types.*)
PHOTOGRAPHER. Thank you! (*Reloads his camera.*)
DAKIS. (*To* GENTLEMAN.) Sign here. (*He signs.*)
PHOTOGRAPHER. (*To* JOE.) Did you get the name?
JOE. (*Writing story in note-book at desk No. 2.*) I got it.
PHOTOGRAPHER. (*Crosses to* JOE.) Park Avenue?
JOE. Spell it backwards.
PHOTOGRAPHER. K-R-A-P.
JOE. You got it. (PHOTOGRAPHER *chortles. They cross up to rail.*)

DAKIS. (*To* GENTLEMAN.) That's all. We'll notify you when to come down to pick up the rest of your property.

GENTLEMAN. (*Plucks out some tickets from his wallet, hands them to* DAKIS.) Excellent work, Officer, excellent! (*Exits* U. L. *with* LADY.)

DAKIS. (*Examines tickets with a slow, mounting burn. To* CALLAHAN.) How do you like that jerk? Two tickets for the *flower* show! There are two kinds of people in this precinct—the crumbs and the elite; and the elite are crumbs. (CALLAHAN, *seated desk No.* 2, *laughs through his nose.* DAKIS *sits down and checks through his " squeals."*)

MCLEOD. (*Typing.*) You might as well go home now, young lady: soon as we finish this we're through.

SUSAN. A few minutes more . . . ? Please!

MCLEOD. (*Sighs. To* ARTHUR.) Weight?

ARTHUR. A hundred and fifty-two.

MCLEOD. Height?

ARTHUR. Five eleven.

MCLEOD. Identifying marks? Scars? Come here! (*Pulls* ARTHUR'S *face around.*) Scar on the left cheek. (*Types.*) And a tattoo. Which arm was that on? (ARTHUR *raises* L. *hand.*) Left? A heart and the name " Joy." (*Phone rings.* CALLAHAN *answers it, desk No.* 2.)

CALLAHAN. 21st Squad, Detectives, Callahan. Yeah? A jumper? Fifty-thoid Street. (MCLEOD *stops typing, listens.*) Her name? Mc . . . ? What . . . ?

MCLEOD. (*Calls across room, sharply.*) What was that name?

CALLAHAN. (*On phone.*) Wait a minute . . . ! (*To* MCLEOD.) What's at, Jim?

MCLEOD. You got a jumper?

CALLAHAN. Yeah.

MCLEOD. Woman?

CALLAHAN. Yeah.

MCLEOD. She killed?

CALLAHAN. Sixteenth floor.

MCLEOD. Who is it?

CALLAHAN. What's a matter with you?

MCLEOD. Who is it?

CALLAHAN. Name is McFadden. Old lady. Her son just identified her. Why?

MCLEOD. (*Mops brow with handkerchief.*) Nothing. That's my street. 53rd. (CALLAHAN *looks at* MCLEOD *with puzzlement, concludes phone conversation sotto voce.*)

SUSAN. (*Standing behind* ARTHUR'S *chair and smiling sadly at* ARTHUR.) A tattoo?

ARTHUR. (*Sheepishly.*) The others all had them. It made me feel like a real sailor. I was *such* a kid. Seven years ago.

SUSAN. Seven? It was yesterday, Jiggs.

ARTHUR. Seven years. Another world.

BRODY. (*Finishes fingerprinting* LEWIS.) Okay, Lewis! Go in there and wash your hands. Next . . . ? (LEWIS *walks to washroom, slowly.*)

MCLEOD. Arthur! (ARTHUR *rises, walks slowly up to* BRODY *at fingerprint board. They exchange glances.*)

BRODY. (*Softly.*) This hand, son. Just relax it. That's it. This finger. Roll it toward me.

DAKIS. (*Rises.*) Well, three old squeals polished off. I'm clean. (*Crosses into* LIEUTENANT'S *office, leaving door open.*)

CALLAHAN. There's one here I'm sure they did. (*Propels himself in swivel chair, over to* CHARLIE, *bench* R.) Charlie, did you burglarize this apartment on 61st Str . . . (*Silence!*) Why don't you give us a break? You help us . . . we'll help you.

CHARLIE. How the hell you gonna help me? I'm a four-time loser. I'm gone to jail for the rest of my life. How the hell you gonna help me?

CALLAHAN. You lived a louse, you wanta die a louse?

CHARLIE. Yes! (CALLAHAN *starts to give him the back of his hand.*) Careful! De sign says courtesy.

CALLAHAN. Coitesy? For you, you bum! You want coitesy? Here! (*Tears off sign on* LIEUTENANT'S *door, hits him on head with it.* CHARLIE *laughs.* LEWIS *comes swaggering out of washroom.*)

BRODY. (*Finishes fingerprinting* ARTHUR.) That's all, son. Go inside and wash your hands. (ARTHUR *goes into washroom.* LEWIS *and* MCLEOD *cross to desk No.* 2.)

MCLEOD. All right, Lewis. . . . Sign here. (BRODY *crosses to table* U. C. CALLAHAN *crosses to files* L.)

SHOPLIFTER. (*Rises, to* SUSAN.) It don't hurt. You roll it. (*Demonstrates.*) Like that. Just gets your hands a little dirty. It washes right off. It's nothing. (SUSAN *crumples into a chair* R. *of desk No.* 1.) What's a matter? Did I say something? (SUSAN *shakes her head.*) Are you married? (SUSAN *shakes head.*) Me neither. Everybody tells you why don't you get married. You should get married. My mother, my father, my sisters, my brother—"Get married!" As if I didn't want to get married. Where do you find a man? Get me a man, I'll marry him. *Anything!* As long as it's got pants. You think I'd be here? A rotten crocodile bag? I'd be home, cooking him such a meal. Get married!!? It's easy to talk! (*Sits again.*)

JOE. (*Crossing with* PHOTOGRAPHER, BARNES *and* CHARLIE *to desk No.* 2. *To* BARNES.) O. K., Steve! Get 'em over here.

BARNES. (*Moves chair for* LEWIS. *Nudges* CHARLIE *with his stick.*) Rise and shine, Charlie. (*They line up in front of desk No.* 2. DAKIS *crosses out of office, puts coat on and sits.* MCLEOD *sits desk No.* 1.)

JOE. (*To* BARNES.) Want to stand on the end? (BARNES *does.*)

BARNES. Stand here, Lewis.

LEWIS. (*Comes close to* CHARLIE, *murmurs in his ear.*) You louse! I ought to kill you.

CHARLIE. (*Mutters.*) Me? The thanks I get!

JOE. (*To* PHOTOGRAPHER.) Wait a minute! I want to line up those bullets. I want 'em in the shot. (*Stands bullets on end.*) Can you get 'em in? (MCLEOD *picks up* ARTHUR'S "*sheet.*" *Crosses to above desk No.* 2.)

PHOTOGRAPHER. Yeah! Ready?

LEWIS. Thirty grand, eh?

CHARLIE. Uh!

LEWIS. I saw the list.

PHOTOGRAPHER. (*To* BARNES, *posing them for the shot.*) Grab him by the arm. Look at him.

CHARLIE. (*Mutters.*) Lists? It's a racket! People get big insurance on fake stuff. They collect on it.

BARNES. (*Smiling for photo, through his gleaming teeth.*) Sh! You spoil the picture. (*FLASH. The picture is taken.* BARNES' *gleaming smile vanishes.*) Over there! (*He waves them to bench* D. R. *with his club, turns to* JOE *to make sure his name is spelled correctly, fixes chair.*)

LEWIS. What about that fourteen hundred dollars?

CHARLIE. (*Indignantly.*) I had it on me for your protection. If this flatfoot had any sense, he was supposed to take it and let us go . . . Dumb cop! Can I help it? (BARNES *crosses, handcuffs them, goes* U. S. *of door of* LIEUTENANT'S *office.*)

LEWIS. Now, look, I want my share.

CHARLIE. All right, Lewis. I'm not gonna argue with you . . . If it'll make you happy, I'll give you the whole fourteen hundred. Satisfied?

LEWIS. (*Thinks it over.*) Ya.

CHARLIE. Good. (ARTHUR *crosses to* MCLEOD.)

BARNES. No talking.

MCLEOD. (*To* ARTHUR.) Your signature. Here! (ARTHUR *glances at card, hesitates.*)

SUSAN. (*Rises.*) Shouldn't he see a lawyer first?

MCLEOD. It's routine.

SUSAN. Anyway, a lawyer should . . . (MCLEOD *presses his temples, annoyed.*)

ARTHUR. Susan! (*Shakes his head.*)

SUSAN. Excuse me. (*Crosses* U. *near* BRODY U. C. MCLEOD *hands* ARTHUR *pen.* ARTHUR *looks about for an ash-tray for his cigarette butt.*)

MCLEOD. On the floor. (ARTHUR *throws it on floor.*) Step on it! (ARTHUR *steps on butt, crosses to* MCLEOD.)

ARTHUR. Where do I sign?

MCLEOD. Here. (*Indicates line on card.* ARTHUR *signs. Sits chair* R. *of desk No. 1. Pause.*)

SUSAN. (*Crossing to* ARTHUR.) I believe in you, Arthur. I want you to know. Deep inside—deep down, no matter what happens—I have faith in you.

JOE. (*To* PHOTOGRAPHER.) Now, this one. (*To* MCLEOD.) You want to be in this?

MCLEOD. (*Pressing his temples.*) No! Got an aspirin, Yussel?

JOE. (*Curtly.*) No. (*Walks away.*)

PHOTOGRAPHER. (*To* ARTHUR.) You mind standing up? (*Flashes picture as* ARTHUR *rises.*)

SUSAN. (*Hysterical. Crosses to* PHOTOGRAPHER, *turns to* BRODY.) No! No! They don't have to do that to him! They don't have to. (*Desperately, to* BRODY.) Officer Brody. They're not going to print that in the papers, are they?

ARTHUR. (*Goes to her* U. L. *at desk No. 2.*) It's all right, Suzy! Stop trembling. Please. I don't care . . .

BRODY. (*Beckons* JOE *and* PHOTOGRAPHER *out through gate* U. L.) Joe! Teeney! (*They follow him off* U. L. *gate.*)

SUSAN. I'm not . . . really . . . It was the sudden flash! (*Buries head in her hands, turns away to control herself.*)

DAKIS. (*Putting on his hat and jacket, to* SHOPLIFTER.) Well, quarter to nine. Night court'll be open by the time we get there. Come on. (*Crosses around desk No.* 2 *to her* L.)

SHOPLIFTER. (*Rising, picking up her bag and scarf.*) What do I do?

DAKIS. They'll tell you. Your brother-in-law's gonna be there, ain't he?

SHOPLIFTER. Yeah. All I can do is thank goodness my sister's sexy. Well . . . (*Looks about.*) So long, everybody! Really it's been very nice meeting you all. And I'm sorry I caused you all this trouble! Good-bye! (*She and* DAKIS *go off* U. L.)

MCLEOD. (*Crossing to* SUSAN.) You better go home now, young lady. It's all over.

SUSAN. May I talk to Arthur? For two minutes, alone? Then I'll go. I won't make any more trouble, I promise.

MCLEOD. All right. (*Handcuffs* ARTHUR *to chair at desk No. 1.*) Two minutes. (*Goes to* LIEUTENANT'S *office, sits in darkened room, in chair above desk.*)

SUSAN. (*Crossing to* ARTHUR, *lips trembling.*) Jiggs . . .

ARTHUR. (*Calming her.*) Don't!

SUSAN. (*At desk No. 1, to* ARTHUR. *Dragging a chair over to him, sits.*) I'm not going to cry. This is no time for emotionalism. I mean we must be calm and wise. We must be realists.

ARTHUR. (*Smiles.*) Yes, Suzy.

SUSAN. The minute I walk out of here, I'm going to call Father.

ARTHUR. No, Susan, don't do that!

SUSAN. But he likes you so much, Arthur. He'll be glad to help.

ARTHUR. I don't want him to know. I'm ashamed. I'm so ashamed of myself.

SUSAN. Jiggs, it's understandable.

ARTHUR. Is it? I don't understand it! I stole, Suzy. I stole money from a man who trusted me! Where am I? Am I still floating around in the middle of the Pacific, looking for concrete platforms that aren't there? How mixed up can you get?

SUSAN. But, Jiggs, everybody gets mixed up, some time or other.

ARTHUR. They don't steal. (*Pause.*) It's a kind of delirium, isn't it?

SUSAN. O. K. So it is delirium, Jiggs. So what? You're coming out of it fine.

ARTHUR. (*Shakes his head.*) Look around, Susan. Look at this. (*Indicates his handcuffs.*) The dreams I had—the plans I made . . . to end like this?

SUSAN. This isn't the end of the world, Jiggs.

ARTHUR. It is for me. How did this happen—how did I come to this? (*Studies handcuffs.*) All I ever wanted was to live quietly in a small college town . . . to study and teach. No! (*Bitterly.*) This isn't a time for study and teachers . . . this is a time for generals.

SUSAN. (*Rises, crossing around chair.*) God, I hate that kind of talk, Jiggs! Everywhere I hear it. . . . I don't believe it. Whatever happens to you, you can still pick up and go on. If ever there was a time for students and teachers, this is it. I know you can still make whatever you choose of your life. (*Pauses, sees his anguish.*) Arthur! Do you want Joy? Would that help? Would you like to see her and talk to her?

ARTHUR. No.

SUSAN. I'll go to Connecticut and bring her back.

ARTHUR. I don't want her.

SUSAN. I'll get her here. Say the word. I'll bring her here, Arthur. She'll come. You know she will.

ARTHUR. I don't want her, Suzy. I don't want Joy.

SUSAN. You're sure?

ARTHUR. Yes. (*Pause.*) I wouldn't know what to say to her now. For five years I've been in love with a girl that doesn't exist. That's finished.

SUSAN. Oh, Arthur! Why couldn't you have fallen in love with *me?*

ARTHUR. (*Looks at her, then, tenderly.*) I've always loved you, Suzy. You were always . . . my baby.

SUSAN. I've news for you. I voted in the last election. I'm years past the age of consent.

ARTHUR. Just an old bag?

SUSAN. Arthur, why didn't you fall in love with me? I'd have been so much better for you. I know I'm not as beautiful as Joy, but . . .

ARTHUR. But you are. Joy's prettier than you, Susan, but you're more beautiful.
SUSAN. Oh, Jiggs, you fracture me! Let us not . . .
ARTHUR. Let us not be emotional. We were going to be realists, remember?
SUSAN. Yes.
ARTHUR. Suzy, when I go to jail . . . (*Her lips quiver again.*) Now . . . Realists?
SUSAN. I'm not going to cry.
ARTHUR. Be my sensible Susan!
SUSAN. Jiggs, I can't be sensible about you. I love you.
ARTHUR. Suzy, darling . . .
SUSAN. Jiggs, whatever happens—when it's over—let's go back home again.
ARTHUR. That would be wonderful, Suzy. That would be everything I ever wanted.
CHARLIE. (*On* D. S. *end of bench down* L. *Pretends to play violin —screeches "Hearts and Flowers." Then laughs raucously.*) Hear that, Lewis? He's facin' five to ten? Wait'll the boys go to work on him. (ARTHUR *and* SUSAN *look at him. To* SUSAN.) What makes you think he'll want you then?
SUSAN. What?
CHARLIE. A kid like this in jail. They toss for him.
SUSAN. What do you mean?
CHARLIE. To see whose chicken he's gonna be! Whose sweetheart!
SUSAN. (*Rises.*) What does that mean? What's he talking about?
ARTHUR. Don't listen to him. (*To* CHARLIE.) Shut up! Who asked you to . . . ?
CHARLIE. After a while you get to like it. Lots a guys come out, they got no use for dames after that.
ARTHUR. Shut up!
CHARLIE. Look at Lewis, there. He's more woman than man, ain't you, ain't you, Lewis? (LEWIS *grins.*)
ARTHUR. (*Rises in a white fury, goes for* CHARLIE, *crossing to* C., *dragging chair to which he is handcuffed.*) Shut up! I'll crack your goddam skull! (BARNES *runs over to* CHARLIE.)
SUSAN. Stop them! Stop! (BRODY *enters quickly,* U. L.) Officer Brody, make him stop! Make him stop!
BRODY. (*To* ARTHUR.) Take it easy! Sit down! (*Kicks* CHARLIE *in shins.*) Why don't you shut up?

SUSAN. Oh, Officer Brody, help us! Help us!

BRODY. (*Crossing to desk No.* 2.) Take it easy. He ain't convicted yet. The Judge might put him on probation. He might get off altogether. A lot of things might happen.

CHARLIE. Yak! Yak!

BRODY. One more peep outa you! One! (*Slaps* CHARLIE. *To* BARNES.) Take them inside! (BARNES *waves* CHARLIE *and* LEWIS *into next room door* D. L. *As they pass* ARTHUR, LEWIS *eyes* ARTHUR *up and down, grinning and nodding.* CHARLIE *hums his mockery of "Hearts and Flowers."* BARNES *prods* CHARLIE *with his night-stick, muttering "We heard the voice." They exit* D. L. *To* SUSAN.) If the complainant still wants to give him a break, that'll help. You got a good lawyer? (*She shakes her head.*) I'll give you the name of a crackerjack! I'm not supposed to, but I'll call him myself. There are a lot of tricks to this business.

SUSAN. Don't let it happen!

BRODY. Here's his picture! (*Crumples up photographic plate, tosses it into waste-basket, goes to his file cabinet* U. R., *fishes out bottle of liquor.* SUSAN *begins to weep.*)

ARTHUR. (*Pulls* SUSAN *to chair* R. *at desk No.* 1.) Sh! Sh! Listen. The rest of my life, I'm going to find ways to make this up to you. I swear. Whatever happens . . . (*Puts arms around her, pulls her down into chair alongside him, holds her tight.*)

SUSAN. (*Clinging to him.*) Arthur, I . . .

ARTHUR. Sh! Don't say anything more, Suzy. We've got a minute left. Let's just sit here like this . . . quietly. (CALLAHAN *exits gate* U. L. SUSAN *starts to speak.*) Sh! Quiet! (*She buries her head in his shoulder, and they sit there in a gentle embrace. After a second's silence, she relaxes.*) Better?

SUSAN. (*Nods.*) Mm!

BRODY. (*Goes into* LIEUTENANT'S *office, looking for* MCLEOD.) What are you sitting in the dark for? (*Switches on light.*) Want a drink, Jim?

MCLEOD. No.

BRODY. (*Pours himself a stiff drink while standing between door and desk No.* 3.) Jim, I've been your partner for thirteen years. I ever ask you for a favor?

MCLEOD. (*Pressing hand to his temples.*) What is it, Lou?

BRODY. That kid outside. (MCLEOD *groans.*) I want you to give him a break.

MCLEOD. You know better. I can't adjudicate this case.
BRODY. And what the hell do you think you're doing?
MCLEOD. What makes him so special?
BRODY. A lot. I think he's a good kid. He's got a lot on the ball. Given another chance . . . (*Pause.*) Jim, he reminds me of my boy.
MCLEOD. Mike?—was a hero.
BRODY. Why? Because he was killed? If Mike'd be alive today, he'd have the same problems this kid has.
MCLEOD. Lou, Lou—how can you compare?
BRODY. Thousands like 'em, I guess. New generation, a new idea. We don't even understand them, Jim. I didn't Mike, till he was killed. (*Pause.*) Too late then. (*Swallows his drink.*) How about it?
MCLEOD. Don't ask me, will you?
BRODY. But I am.
MCLEOD. (*Rises, pushing chair back* U. C.) I can't. I can't do it, Lou. I can't drop the charges.
BRODY. Louder, please! I don't seem to hear so good outa this ear.
MCLEOD. This fellow and Mike—day and night—there's no comparison.
BRODY. Jim, this is me, Lou Brody. Remember me? What do you mean you can't drop it? You coulda let him go two hours ago. You still can. The complainant left it up to you. I heard him.
MCLEOD. Be logical, Lou.
BRODY. To hell with logic! I see you logic the life out of a thing. Heart! Heart! The world's crying for a little heart. (*Pause.*) What do you say?
MCLEOD. No, Lou. No dice!
BRODY. (*Crosses to* D. S. *chair, sits.*) My partner! Arrest his own mother.
MCLEOD. I'm too old to start compromising now.
BRODY. There's a full moon out tonight. It shows in your puss.
MCLEOD. (*Crossing a step* L.) You shouldn't drink so much, Lou. It melts the lining of your brain.
BRODY. (*Pushes bottle to him.*) Here! You take it. Maybe that's what you need. Maybe it'll melt that rock you got in there for a heart.
MCLEOD. Stop it, Lou, will you? My nerves are like banjo strings.

BRODY. Well, play something on them. Play "Love's Old Sweet Song."

MCLEOD. (*Crossing to* BRODY.) Shut up! Lay off! God damn it! I'm warning you. Lay off! (*Silence.*)

BRODY. (*Studies him, then . . . softer.*) What's the matter?

MCLEOD. I'm drowning, Lou. I'm drowning. That's all. I'm drowning in my own juices. (*Sits in swivel.* JOE *enters* U. L.)

BRODY. I wish I could understand what makes you tick.

MCLEOD. (*As* JOE *enters* LIEUTENANT'S *office.*) I don't expect you to understand me, Lou. I know I'm different than the others. I think differently. I'm not a little boy who won't grow up, playing cops and robbers all his life, like Callahan; and I'm not an insurance salesman, like you, Lou. I'm here out of principle!! Principle, Lou. All my life I've lived according to principle! And I couldn't deviate even if I wanted to.

BRODY. Sometimes you gotta bend with the wind . . . or break! Be a little human, Jim! Don't be such a friggin' monument!

MCLEOD. How, how? How do you compromise? How do you compromise—convictions that go back to the roots of your childhood? I hate softness. I don't believe in it. My mother was soft: It killed her. I'm no Christian. I don't believe in the other cheek. I hate mushiness. You ask me to compromise for this kid? Who the hell is he? Now, right now, Lou, I'm faced with a problem of my own that's ripping me up like a 22 bullet bouncing around inside, and I can't compromise on that. So what do I do? What do I do?

JOE. Try picking up that phone and calling her.

MCLEOD. Who?

JOE. Mary. (*Tosses aspirin box onto desk.*) Here's your aspirin.

MCLEOD. What are you talking about?

JOE. This "22 bullet."

MCLEOD. You don't know anything about it.

JOE. It's one story I had in my pocket years before it happened.

MCLEOD. Listening at keyholes, Yussel?

JOE. No. I met Mary years before you did. The spring of '41—I was on the *Newark Star*. She didn't remember me. I never forgot her, though. It's one of those faces you don't forget. She's one in a million, your Mary. I know. She's a fine girl, Seamus. She could have had anything she wanted—materially—anything. She chose you instead. Why? What'd you have to offer her? Buttons!—

These crazy hours, this crazy life? She loves you. You don't know how lucky you are. I know. I'm little and ugly—and because I'm a lover of beauty, I'm going to live and die alone. But you? . . . the jewel was placed in your hands. Don't throw it away. You'll never get it back again! (CALLAHAN *re-enters* U. L. *squad room. Offers* ARTHUR *and* SUSAN, D. L., *cigarettes and lights them for them.*)

BRODY. (*Soft.*) You know what you were like before you met Mary? You remember?

MCLEOD. Yes.

BRODY. Like a stick! Thin.

MCLEOD. (*Broken.*) Yes.

BRODY. Dried up, lonely, cold.

MCLEOD. Yes.

BRODY. And you know what tenderness and warmth she brought to your life?

MCLEOD. I know. I know better than you. (MARY *enters* U. L.)

BRODY. So what the hell you asking me what to do? Pick up the phone! Get on your knees. Crawl!

CALLAHAN. Yes, Miss?

MARY. Is Detective McLeod here?

CALLAHAN. He's busy, Miss.

MARY. (*Wearily.*) It's *Mrs.*, Mrs. McLeod.

CALLAHAN. Oh! Yes, ma'am. I'll tell him you're here. (*Crosses. Pokes his head into* LIEUTENANT'S *office, to* MCLEOD.) Jim, your wife is out here. (MCLEOD *rises at once, comes out of* LIEUTENANT'S *office, to* MARY. JOE *and* BRODY *follow him out, discreetly vanish into washroom.* BRODY *leaves whisky bottle and glass on file* U. R. *near washroom door.*)

MARY. (*Digs into her purse to avoid his eyes. Her voice low, brittle, weary.*) I'm leaving now, Jim. I thought I'd come up and tell you. Here are the keys.

MCLEOD. (*Softly.*) Come inside.

MARY. My taxi's waiting.

MCLEOD. Send it away.

MARY. No. My things are in it.

MCLEOD. What things?

MARY. My valises and my trunk.

MCLEOD. Oh, Mary, be sensible.

MARY. I intend to. Let's not drag it out, Jim! Please! I don't want any more arguments. I can't stand them. (*Her voice becomes shrill.* CALLAHAN *passes by, crosses to files* D. L. *She clamps controls on, becoming almost inaudible.*) It's only going to make things worse.

MCLEOD. Come inside! I can't talk to you here.

MARY. The meter's ticking.

MCLEOD. (*Firmly.*) Let it tick! Come! (*She goes into* LIEUTENANT'S *office with him. He shuts door, turns to her.*) Mary, this isn't the time or place to discuss our lives, past, present or future. I want you to take your things and go home. I'll be back at eight A. M. and we'll work this out then.

MARY. You think we can?

MCLEOD. We'll have to.

MARY. I don't think it's possible.

MCLEOD. Wait a minute! Wait one minute! I don't get this. What are *you* so bitter about? Who's to blame for tonight? You put me in a cement mixer. And now you're acting as if I were the . . .

MARY. The whore?

MCLEOD. Don't say that!

MARY. I didn't invent the word, either, Jim.

MCLEOD. I wasn't myself.

MARY. You were never more yourself, Jim, and you called me a whore. (*Pause.*)

MCLEOD. I'm sorry, Mary.

MARY. It's all right. I'm beyond feeling. I'm nice and numb.

MCLEOD. You're certainly in no condition to discuss this tonight.

MARY. I've thought everything over and over and over again and I don't see any other way out. I know what I'm doing has got to be. Our life is finished. We couldn't go on from here.

MCLEOD. You're married to me. You can't just walk out. Marriage is a sacrament, Mary. You don't dissolve it like that.

MARY. You once told me when you bring a married prostitute in here, if she's convicted, her marriage can be dissolved "just" like that! Well, I've been brought in and I've been convicted.

MCLEOD. I don't like that talk. Stop that talk, will you, Mary? I'm trying, I'm trying . . .

MARY. To what?

MCLEOD. To put all this behind me.

MARY. But you can't do it? Can you?

MCLEOD. If you'll let me.

MARY. Me? What have I got to say about it? I know the way your mind works. It never lets go. The rest of our days we'll be living with this. If you won't be saying it, you'll be thinking it. (*Pause.*) It's no good. It won't work. I don't want to live a cat-and-dog existence. I couldn't take it. I'd dry up. I'd dry up and die.

MCLEOD. Why didn't you ever tell me? If you'd come to me once, just once . . .

MARY. What good would it have done? Would you have understood? Would you have been able to forgive me?

MCLEOD. Wasn't I entitled to know?

MARY. Yes, yes!

MCLEOD. Why didn't you tell me?

MARY. Jim, I can't go over this again and again and again. I refuse to.

MCLEOD. If I didn't love you and need you so, it'd be simple, you understand?

MARY. I understand.

MCLEOD. Simple. You go home now and wait till morning.

MARY. That won't help us. Please, I'm so tired, let me go now, Jim.

MCLEOD. To what? What'll you go to? You, who turn on every light in the house when I'm not there!

MARY. Let me go, Jim.

MCLEOD. You, who can't fall asleep unless my arms are around you! Where will you go?

MARY. Jim, I beg you . . .

MCLEOD. No, Mary, I'm not going to. (*Grasps her by the arm.*)

MARY. You're hurting my arm.

MCLEOD. I'm sorry . . . I'm sorry. (*Lets her go.*)

MARY. You ripped my sleeve.

MCLEOD. You'll sew it up.

MARY. The taxi's waiting. Please, Jim, let me go, without any more razor-slashing. I hate it.

MCLEOD. You'd go without a tear? (CALLAHAN *starts to cross from* D. L. *to* LIEUTENANT'S *office.*)

MARY. I wouldn't say that. One or two, perhaps. I haven't many left. You'll find them all on my pillow.

MCLEOD. Mary, I . . . (CALLAHAN *enters* LIEUTENANT'S *office, leaving paper on desk No. 3, exits. Crosses back to files* D. L.) Mary, you just don't stop loving someone.

MARY. I wouldn't have thought so. I wouldn't have believed it could happen. But there it is. I suppose in this life we all die many times before they finally bury us. This was one of those deaths. Sudden, unexpected, like being run over by a bus. It happens.

MCLEOD. (*Turns her.*) Who do you think you're kidding?

MARY. No one! (*Begins to cry.*) Least of all, myself.

MCLEOD. (*Takes her in his arms.*) Mary, I love you.

MARY. (*Clinging to him, sobbing.*) Then help me! I'm trying to be a human being. I'm trying to bundle myself together. It took every bit of strength to go this far. Help me, Jim. (CALLAHAN *crosses to files* U. R.)

MCLEOD. It's no use, sweetheart, it's no use. I couldn't go home if you weren't waiting for me with the radio going and the smell of coffee on the stove. I'd blow out my brains. I would, Mary, if I went home to an empty flat—I wouldn't dare take my gun with me. Now powder your nose! Put on some lipstick. (*She kisses him.* SIMS *appears at gate, outside of rail* U. L.)

CALLAHAN. (*Crosses to* SIMS *at gate* U. L.) Yes, Counsellor?

SIMS. I want to see Detective McLeod.

CALLAHAN. All right, Counsellor. Come in. (*Knocks on* LIEUTENANT'S *office door, crosses to files* U. R.)

MCLEOD. Come in!

CALLAHAN. Someone's outside to see you.

MARY. I'll go home, now.

MCLEOD. No. Wait a minute.

MARY. (*Smiles now.*) That taxi bill is going to break us.

MCLEOD. (*Grins back at her.*) Let it break us, what do we care? It's only money. (*He goes out to squad room, sees* SIMS, *his face goes grim again. Crosses to* SIMS.) You see, Counsellor? I told you your client was acting.

SIMS. He's still in shock.

MCLEOD. He'll be okay in the morning.

SIMS. (*Crossing to* D. C.) I suppose so. No thanks to you. When he's brought back here tomorrow, though, he'd better remain okay. This is not to happen again! You're not to lay a finger on him. If you do . . .

MCLEOD. (*Crossing to* SIMS.) Then advise him again to keep his mouth shut.

SIMS. You're lucky you're not facing a murder charge yourself, right now.
MCLEOD. I could always get you to defend me.
SIMS. And I probably would. That's my job, no matter how I feel personally.
MCLEOD. As long as you get your fee?
SIMS. I've defended many men at my own expense.
MCLEOD. That was very noble of you.
SIMS. Nobility doesn't enter into it. Every man has a right to counsel, no matter how guilty he might seem to you, or to me, for that matter. Every man has a right not to be arbitrarily judged, particularly by men in authority; not by you, not by the Congress, not even by the President of the United States. The theory being these human rights are derived from God Himself.
MCLEOD. I know the theory, Counsellor. (BARNES, CHARLIE *and* LEWIS *enter* D. L. CHARLIE *sits bench down* R. LEWIS *and* BARNES *at table* U. C.)
SIMS. But you don't go along with it? Well, you're not alone. There are others. You've a lot of friends all over the world. Read the headlines. But don't take it on yourself to settle it. Let history do that.
MCLEOD. Save it for the Fourth of July, Counsellor.
SIMS. I'll save it for the Commissioner. I intend to see him about you. I'm not going to let you get away with this.
MCLEOD. As long as Schneider gets away with it, Counsellor, all's well. Why do you take cases like this, if you're so high-minded? Schneider killed the Harris girl—he's guilty. You know it as well as I do.
SIMS. I don't know it. I don't even permit myself to speculate on his guilt or innocence. The moment I do that, I'm judging . . . and it is not my job to judge. My job is to defend my client, not to judge him. That remains with the courts. (*Turns to go toward gate* U. L.)
MCLEOD. And you've got that taken care of, Counsellor. Between bought witnesses and perjured testimony . . . (SIMS *stops in his tracks, turns to* MCLEOD.)
SIMS. If you're so set on hanging Schneider, why don't you ask Mrs. McLeod if she can supply a corroborating witness?!! (MCLEOD *looks a little sick. Lights a cigarette slowly. Returns to* LIEUTENANT'S *office.*)

MARY. What's the matter, dear?
MCLEOD. Nothing.
MARY. This has been our black day.
MCLEOD. Yes.
MARY. I'm sorry, darling. And yet, in a way, I'm glad it's out in the open. This has been hanging over my head so long. I've had such a terrible feeling of guilt all the time.
MCLEOD. (*Mutters.*) All right! All right!
MARY. I needed help and there was no one. I couldn't even go to my parents.
MCLEOD. They didn't know?
MARY. No.
MCLEOD. You didn't tell them?
MARY. I didn't dare. I didn't want to hurt them. You know how sweet and simple they are.
MCLEOD. You didn't go home then?
MARY. No.
MCLEOD. Where'd you go?
MARY. That's when I came to New York.
MCLEOD. And how long was that before I met you, Mary?
MARY. Two years.
MCLEOD. Who'd you go with then?
MARY. No one.
MCLEOD. How many others were there, Mary?
MARY. Others?
MCLEOD. How many other men?
MARY. None. (*Alarmed now at look on his face.*) What's the matter with you, Jim?
MCLEOD. Wait a minute! Wait a minute!
MARY. No! What's the matter with you?
MCLEOD. At an autopsy I witnessed yesterday, the medical examiner sawed off the top of a man's skull, took out the brain, and held it in his hand. (*Holds out his hand.*) Like that.
MARY. (*Horrified.*) Why are you telling me this?
MCLEOD. Because I'd give everything I own to be able to take out my brain and hold it under the faucet and wash away the dirty pictures you put there tonight.
MARY. Dirty pictures?
MCLEOD. Yes!
MARY. Oh! I see. (*Long pause.*) I see. (*To herself.*) Yes. That

would be convenient, if we could. (*She straightens out, turns to him.*) But when you wash away what I may have put there, you'll find you've a rotten spot in your brain, Jim, and it's growing. I know. I've watched it . . .

MCLEOD. (*Hoarsely.*) Mary! That's enough.

MARY. (*Stronger than he, at last.*) No, let's have the truth! I could never find it in my heart to acknowledge one tiny flaw in you—because I loved you so—and God help me, I still do!—But let's have the truth, for once, wherever it may lead. You think you're on the side of the angels? You're not! You haven't even a drop of ordinary human forgiveness in your whole nature. You're everything you've always said you hated in your own father.

MCLEOD. (*Throws on his jacket, takes her by arm.*) I'm not going to let you wander off in the streets this way. I'm going to take you home myself.

MARY. (*Screams at him.*) What for? To kill me the way your father killed your mother!! There are the keys. (*He takes his hand off her as if he'd been struck. She puts keys down on desk, turns to go off through squad room and door* U. L.)

MCLEOD. Where are you going? (*Pause. She looks at him, sadly.*)

MARY. Far away . . . you won't find me. I'm scorching my earth . . . burning my cities.

MCLEOD. When will I see you?

MARY. Never. . . . Good-bye. . . . (*She goes through squad room and off* U. L. MCLEOD, *dazed, walks slowly back to squad room.*)

BRODY. (*Enters washroom with* JOE.) How'd it go?

MCLEOD. Fine.

BRODY. I mean Mary.

MCLEOD. Fine. Dandy. (*Crossing to* SUSAN.) All right, young lady, your two minutes are up. (LIEUTENANT *enters* D. L.)

LIEUTENANT. (*To* MCLEOD.) What the hell's the matter with you?

MCLEOD. Nothing. . . .

LIEUTENANT. Don't you feel well?

MCLEOD. Yes, sir. Feel all right.

LIEUTENANT. (*To* BRODY.) Am I crazy? Look at him.

BRODY. You've gone all green, Jim.

MCLEOD. I've got a headache.

LIEUTENANT. You better go home. Buzz your doctor.

MCLEOD. I've got a squeal to finish off, Lieutenant.

LIEUTENANT. Brody! You finish it off.
BRODY. (*Reluctantly.*) Yes, sir.
MCLEOD. I'd rather do it myself.
LIEUTENANT. You go home. That's an order.
MCLEOD. Yes, sir.
LIEUTENANT. Callahan! You catch for Jim tonight.
CALLAHAN. Yes, sir. (*Crosses up to duty chart, takes it off wall.*)
BRODY. (*Crossing to* MCLEOD.) What happened, Jim? What's wrong?
MCLEOD. (*Sits heavily,* L. *of desk No.* 2.) Mary left me. Walked out. We're finished.
BRODY. Too bad. She'll come back.
MCLEOD. No. . . . This was for keeps. (LIEUTENANT *crosses to* L.)
LIEUTENANT. What are you sitting there for? Why don't you go home? (LIEUTENANT *exits* D. L.)
MCLEOD. Because I haven't got any . . .
JOE. (*Comes down to him, close.*) You drove her away, didn't you? Why? (MCLEOD *doesn't answer.*) I tried to warn you, you damn fool. Why?
MCLEOD. Why? Why do we do these things, Yussel? Who knows? I built my whole life on hating my father—and all the time he was inside me laughing—or maybe he was crying, the poor bastard! Maybe he couldn't help himself, either. (*An excited woman,* INDIGNANT CITIZEN, *enters,* U. L.)
CALLAHAN. Yes, Miss? (*He is at desk No.* 2, *reaching into bottom drawer for celluloid letters to replace name on duty chart.*)
INDIGNANT CITIZEN. Someone snatched my purse . . .
CALLAHAN. Come on in, Miss. We'll take care of you. (*Bends over to pick up a letter.*)
INDIGNANT CITIZEN. This happened to me once before . . . on 72nd Street . . . (CHARLIE *lunges for* CALLAHAN'S *exposed gun, grabs it, hits* CALLAHAN *on head with butt, knocking him out.* BARNES *raises his club.*)
CHARLIE. Drop that club! (*Aims at* BARNES.)
BRODY. Drop it! He's a four-time loser. He'll kill you. (BARNES *drops club.*)
CHARLIE. Goddamn right. Rot in jail the rest of my life! I take five or six a-you bastards with me first. (BARNES *makes a movement.*)

BRODY. Take it easy! He can't get by the desk.

CHARLIE. Shut up. One word! One move! Anybody! (MCLEOD, *seated* C., *laughs*.)

MCLEOD. I was wondering when you'd get around to it, Charlie.

CHARLIE. None of your guff, you!!

MCLEOD. Give me that gun! (*Rises*.)

CHARLIE. In the gut . . . you'll get it. One step! I'm warnin' you. One!

BRODY. Easy, Jim. He can't get by the desk.

MCLEOD. (*Walks toward him, reaching for gun*.) You evil son of a bitch! (CHARLIE *fires point-blank at* MCLEOD. *One, two, three quick shots*. MCLEOD *staggers back and is whirled around by impact*. BARNES *goes into action, knocks gun out of* CHARLIE'S *hand, starts beating him over the head with his club*. O'BRIEN *crosses to* CHARLIE. KEOGH *and* MOTORCYCLE COP *rush in*.)

BRODY. (*Rushes to him, puts arms around him, supporting him*.) Jim! Did he get you? Are you hurt? (CALLAHAN *crosses to washroom*.)

MCLEOD. Slightly. . . . (*A little boy for one second*.) Oh, Mary, Mary, Mary . . . Slightly killed, I should say. . . . (LIEUTENANT *comes running in from door* D. L., *also a number of* POLICEMEN *crowd in from* U. L. GALLAGHER *in with* LIEUTENANT.)

LIEUTENANT. What's happened?

BARNES. That son-of-a-bitch shot Jim . . .

LIEUTENANT. Take him inside! Get him into bed, quick.

BRODY. (*To* MCLEOD.) Easy, baby. Come, I'll carry you to bed. . . .

MCLEOD. Wait a minute.

BRODY. Now, Jim.

MCLEOD. No. Don't! Don't pull at me. . . . (*Sinks back into a chair* L. *of desk No*. 2.)

JOE. You got to lie down, Seamus.

MCLEOD. No. Once I lay down I'm not going to get up again.

LIEUTENANT. Notify the Communication Bureau. Get an ambulance. Quick!

MCLEOD. Never mind the doctor! Get a priest.

BRODY. Feel that bad, Jim? (GALLAGHER *goes to phone desk No*. 2.)

GALLAGHER. (*On phone*.) Communication Bureau.

LIEUTENANT. Why don't you lie down, Jim?

MCLEOD. Get me a drink.
LIEUTENANT. (*To* BRODY.) With a belly wound . . . ?
BRODY. (*Whispers.*) What difference does it make? . . . Look at him! (LIEUTENANT *nods—goes for glass of whisky on files up* R.)
MCLEOD. Don't whisper, Lou. I can hear you.
BRODY. Sure you can. You're all right, baby. They can't hurt you. You're one of the indestructibles; you're immortal, baby.
MCLEOD. Almost, Lou. Almost. Don't rush me. Give me your hand, Lou. Squeeze! Harder! (SUSAN *begins to sob.*)
ARTHUR. Don't cry, Suzy. Don't cry! (CALLAHAN *crosses to* CHARLIE, *drags him off.*)
MCLEOD. (*Glances up at* ARTHUR, *shakes head. To* BRODY.) Give me Buster's prints! I don't know. I hope you're right, Lou. Maybe he'll come in tomorrow with a murder rap. I don't know any more. Get me his prints. (BRODY *goes for them.* CHARLIE *is dragged off* U. L. *by* O'BRIEN *and* BARNES, *half unconscious, moaning.*)
JOE. How're you feeling, Seamus?
MCLEOD. Yussel! Find her! Ask her to forgive me. And help her. She needs help . . . will you?
JOE. Sure. Now take it easy. (BRODY *hands* ARTHUR'S *fingerprint sheet to* MCLEOD, *who tears it up. Looks at* LIEUTENANT.)
MCLEOD. Tear 'em up. Unchain him, Lou. The keys are in my pocket. We have no case here, Lieutenant. The complainant withdrew. (*Crosses himself.*) In the name of the Father and the Son and the Holy Ghost. Oh, my God! I'm heartily sorry for having offended Thee. I detest all my sins because I dread the loss of Heaven . . . (*Falls.* BRODY *catches him, eases him to the ground, feels for his pulse.*)
BRODY. He's gone!
JOE. (*Also kneeling.*) He's dead.
LIEUTENANT. (*Completes prayer.*) "I firmly resolve with the help of Thy Grace to confess my sins, to do penance and to amend my life. Amen." (*Crosses himself.*)
BRODY. (*Murmurs.*) Amen. (BARNES *uncovers, crosses himself.* BRODY *crosses himself, rises clumsily, goes to* ARTHUR, *unlocks his handcuffs.*) All right, son. Go on home. Don't make a monkey outa me! If I see you . . . up here again, I'll kick the guts outa you. Don't make a monkey outa me!

ARTHUR. Don't worry! I won't.

SUSAN. He won't.

BRODY. Get the hell outa here.

SUSAN. Thank you. (SUSAN *takes* ARTHUR'S *hand. They go off* U. L.)

GALLAGHER. (*On phone.*) St. Vincent's? Will you please send a priest over to the 21st Precinct Police Station to administer last rites?

LIEUTENANT. (*On phone.*) Communication Bureau? Notify—the Commissioner—the D. A., the Homicide Squad—21st Precinct. . . . Detective shot . . . killed.

CURTAIN

WORKING PROP PLOT—DETECTIVE STORY

ACT I

Desk No. 1

Swivel chair back of desk
Chair front of desk
Chair U. S. of desk
Typewriter with form—Act I, Act II, Act III
Police forms in drawer
Pads
Envelopes in up top drawer of desk (brown)
Pencils
Newspaper
Gooseneck lamp
New York News comics (Sunday)

Desk No. 2

Swivel chair back of desk
Chair front of desk
Coca-cola bottle—half filled
Ash-tray
Chair D. S. of desk
Two telephones
Waste-basket under desk
Clip board
Pencils
Pads
Police forms in desk
Letters for duty board—L. D. S. drawer
Aspirin box—U. S. T. drawer

LIEUTENANT'S *Office—Desk No. 3*

Swivel chair back of desk
Chair L. of desk
Chair D. L. corner of set
Telephone
Waste-basket under desk
Razor R. top drawer
Shaving cream R. top drawer
Brush R. top drawer
Towel R. top drawer
Lieutenant Act I
Large address book L. top drawer
Cigars C. drawer
Matches C. drawer
Gooseneck lamp
Police forms
Ash-tray

LIEUTENANT'S *Office*

Glass of water on cooler half-filled—Act I, Act II

Water cooler—D. S. R. door

Courtesy card on door to squad room

Filing cabinets with forms below water cooler

Filing cabinets with forms UP S. C. wall

Coat tree R. of window

Off Stage L.

Broom (Willy)

Camera (Photographer)

Flashbulbs (4 every performance) (Photographer)

Four containers of coffee (Brody)

Two sandwiches (Brody)

Four pairs of handcuffs (Barnes, Charlie, Lewis, McLeod)

Old paper files wrapped (McLeod)

Used photo plate (Brody)

Bags of loot—silverware, jewel box with jewels, etc., etc.

Pair of old pants (Charlie)

Coats and suits (loot)

32 revolver, loaded (cover)

Jimmy, 22 revolver with fake bullets

Radio (loot)

Two fur coats (loot)

Four miscellaneous fur pieces (loot)

Eight guns (Detectives)

Eight holsters (Detectives)

Shoulder holster (Lieutenant)

Four sets of keys (Mary, Lieutenant, Arthur)

Fountain pen (McLeod)

Pencils

Badge and case (McLeod)

Address book (Arthur)

Notebook (McLeod)

Lipstick (Mary)

Vanity case (Mary)

Brown briefcase with pictures of Kurt (Sims)

Calling cards (Sims)

Wallet (Arthur)

Coins (Arthur)

Pocket knife (Arthur)

Cigarettes (Detectives)

Cigars (Feinson and Lieutenant)

Book matches (Stork Club—Arthur)

Pawn tickets (Susan and Arthur)

Two parking tickets (Callahan and Dakis)

Large roll of money—$1400 (Charlie)

Roll of money—$120 (Susan)

Two newspapers (Sims and Feinson)

Aspirin box (Feinson)

Water pail—rise of Act II (Willy)

Jewel box with jewelry (loot)

Fingerprint card—Charlie's record (Gus)

Two handkerchiefs (Mary and Mrs. Bagatelle)

All detectives wear guns and holsters. Detective Callahan wears gun loaded with blanks for Act III.

Washroom

Wet towel

Water glass—half filled

Toilet—wash bowl

On door, a towel

u. s. *of Desk No. 1*

Fingerprint board
Fingerprint outfit
Blank fingerprint cards
Small wall-light over board
Under fingerprint board, wastebasket
Height chart

u. s. c.

Large table
Two chairs front of table
On table, wire basket with police forms, newspaper, miscellaneous papers

u. s. r. *Wall*

Filing cabinet with cards
Bottle of whisky (u. s. lower drawer)
Whisky glass (u. s. lower drawer)
Small bench outside of rail—u. l.
Small bench r. of desk No. 2

u. s. l. *Wall*

Filing cabinet with filing cards

On Wall

Calendar
Clipboard r. over filing cabinet
Duty board with names—*At Rise:* Gallagher and Dakis—McLeod changes to McLeod and Brody in Act I
Large bulletin board with pictures of criminals and missing persons, etc., etc. (l. of fingerprint board)
Large electric clock—wall u. c.

Strike—Act I

Water glass on desk No. 1
Containers of coffee
Sandwiches
Wallet, keys, coins, pawn ticket, knife, desk No. 3
22 revolver with fake bullets
Jimmy
Move one of u. s. chairs down to u. s. of desk No. 2

Strike—Act II

Bundle of old files, desk No. 2
Move loot to large table u. c., except jewel box
Place 22 revolver, fake bullets and jimmy on desks No. 2 and No. 3
Place fingerprint card desk No. 2
2 suitcases

Act III

d. r. chair in Lieutenant's office, spotted above Lieutenant's desk No. 3

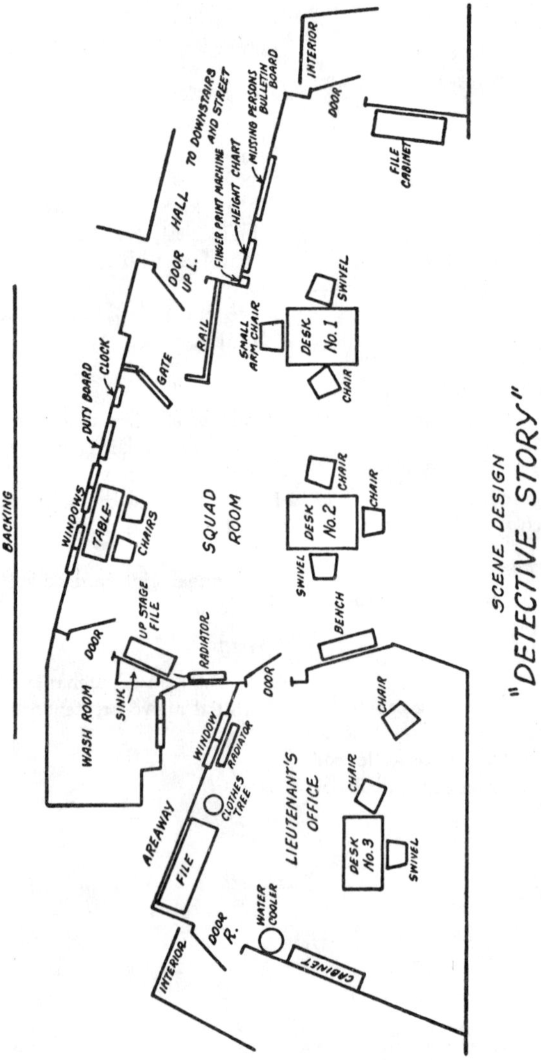
SCENE DESIGN
"DETECTIVE STORY"
BACKING
WASH ROOM
SINK
DOOR
UP STAGE FILE
RADIATOR
WINDOWS
TABLE
CHAIRS
DUTY BOARD
CLOCK
GATE
RAIL
DOOR UP L.
HALL
TO DOWNSTAIRS AND STREET
FINGER PRINT MACHINE
HEIGHT CHART
MISSING PERSONS BULLETIN BOARD
INTERIOR
DOOR
FILE CABINET
SQUAD ROOM
SMALL ARM CHAIR
DESK No. 1
SWIVEL
CHAIR
DESK No. 2
CHAIR
CHAIR
SWIVEL
BENCH
DOOR
WINDOW
RADIATOR
CLOTHES TREE
AREAWAY
FILE
LIEUTENANT'S OFFICE
CHAIR
CHAIR
DESK No. 3
SWIVEL
WATER COOLER
DOOR R.
INTERIOR
CABINET